CAMELBACK

SACRED MOUNTAIN OF PHOENIX

BY GARY DRIGGS

THE FIRST COLLECTION OF STORIES, EXPERIENCES,
PHOTOGRAPHY AND ART RELATING THE STORY OF
OUR SPLENDID FRIEND—CAMELBACK MOUNTAIN.

ARIZONA HISTORICAL FOUNDATION
ARIZONA STATE UNIVERSITY
TEMPE, AZ
1998

To my wife, Kay, and children, Rebecca, Taylor, Kimberly and Benjamin, who have been willing to share my love for Camelback and interest in mountains everywhere.

Mexican gold poppies at the nose of Camelback.
Photo by J.R. Norton.

CAMELBACK
SACRED MOUNTAIN OF PHOENIX

By Gary Driggs

OPPOSITE PAGE: *Climbing the Slab. Photo by J.R. Norton.*

Hiking to the top of Camelback. Photo by Jeff Kida.

Library of Congress Cataloging-in-Publication Data
Driggs, Gary.
Camelback: Sacred Mountain of Phoenix.
Includes bibliographical references.
ISBN 0-910152-17-9
Camelback Mountain—Phoenix history—Arizona flora and fauna.
Library of Congress Catalog Card Number: 98-88616.

Printed in Phoenix, Arizona by environmentally responsive Dryography™ and waterless printing processes.
Second Printing. 2003

C ONTENT S

FOREWORD

By Barry Goldwater
1909—1998

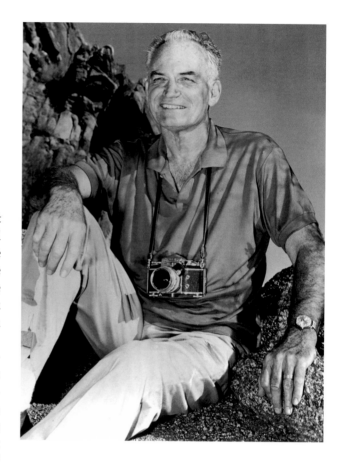

I've spent a good part of my adult life looking at Camelback Mountain. I built my home on a small hill overlooking the north side of Echo Canyon and the Head of Camelback Mountain. Every day I watch the changing moods of Camelback. The colors change as the sun moves across the sky. The red rocks of Camelback remind me of the rocks of the Colorado Plateau, which have been such an important part of my life.

I had a lot of wonderful experiences in both business and civic life. It was both an honor and pleasure to serve in the U.S. Senate and run for the presidency, but one of the things I am most proud of is the work Maggie Kober and I did to help preserve the top of Camelback for a city park. Of course, that effort was only made possible through the efforts of thousands of schoolchildren, volunteers, civic leaders and others who worked to gather both the money and public support.

I've visited and photographed every part of Arizona. My favorite place has been the Colorado River and the Grand Canyon. The experiences I had running the river and hiking the canyon rank at the top of lots of memorable outdoor experiences. But after the Colorado and its canyons I rank the beauty of Camelback right up there with the best spots in Arizona.

When I was first running for the Senate, I took a break from campaigning to take my son and his Cub Scout den on a hike to Havasupai Falls in the Grand Canyon. I asked Gary Driggs to come along with me to help keep all those Cub Scouts under control. We had a great time together and we got the Cubs back safely after a more than 20-mile hike. I took a picture of Gary and gave it to his dad Douglas, who had been a great friend of mine for many years.

Later, Gary made some good suggestions regarding Echo Canyon when we were working on the Save Camelback effort. I'm glad he followed up on those ideas when his brother John became mayor.

I supported John Driggs when he ran for mayor of Phoenix and wrote a letter advocating his election, which was published in *The Arizona Republic*. John was the Charter Government candidate and I was confident he would make a good mayor. I got my start in politics as a Charter Government candidate for the Phoenix City Council. I'm happy that support may have helped get Echo Canyon set aside later as a city park.

This history of Camelback by Gary records the exciting story of Camelback that needs to be more widely known. It helps us appreciate what a fabulous asset Camelback really is. If we had understood all these things earlier, more of Camelback would have been preserved. I hope this book will help more people appreciate what a great heritage we have in Arizona and how we need to work to preserve both the land and its history. I'm also glad that the Arizona Historical Foundation, which I helped found, is publishing this important work.

Barry M. Goldwater
January 1, 1997

ABOVE: *Watercolor by Gunnar Widforss (1879-1934) Camelback from the southwest.* BELOW: *Gary Driggs. Photo by Barry Goldwater in Havasupai Canyon in 1952.* LEFT: *Barry Goldwater on Camelback, circa 1965. Arizona Historical Foundation, University Libraries, Arizona State University.*

GUNNAR WIDFORSS

Gunnar Widforss was born on Oct. 21, 1879, in Stockholm, Sweden. In 1896 he started at the Royal Technical Institute in Stockholm. In 1921 he visited California and was so impressed by the scenery he decided to stay in America. In 1924, he had a one-man exhibition at the National Gallery of Art in Washington consisting of 72 watercolors of Yellowstone, Bryce, Zion, Yosemite and the Grand Canyon. National Gallery Museum Director W.H. Holmes said, "He is possibly the greatest watercolorist in America today." The National Gallery exhibition made Widforss an established painter. He died at the Grand Canyon on November 30, 1934. He is buried at the Canyon, where a 7,800-foot prominence on the North Rim of the Grand Canyon has been designated as Widforss Point in memory of the artist.

INTRODUCTION

BY GARY AVEY

This land that we now call Arizona is truly blessed with a vibrant and diverse panorama of scenic grandeur. Within the state's 113,000 square miles, residents and visitors bask in awe over a canyon so grand that all of New England could reside within its chasms.

In fact, Arizona is home to fourteen national parks and monuments, as well as numerous state parks. When I served as editor of *Arizona Highways* magazine, it was clear that the appreciation for the beauty of Arizona is worldwide.

Amidst this vast array of spectacular landscape, is a relatively neglected treasure—Camelback Mountain. Of course, we all know it well as a landmark, being a magnet for resort developers and homeowners seeking spectacular views. It certainly was the most prominent among the mountains that encircled the original boundaries of Phoenix a century ago.

While Camelback is one of the most popular hiking destinations in metropolitan Phoenix, most hikers and even residents know relatively little about either the natural or human history of the mountain. In short, we love Camelback as a landmark but we take it for granted.

As I have hiked the mountain with Gary, I came to learn new things about Camelback. This was quite surprising, as I have spent a lifetime communicating through publishing the beauty and history of Arizona. I was unaware that Camelback's story had never been published.

Gary Driggs has been working in earnest on recording the history of Camelback for the past three years. During that time, he has taken photographers to every part of the mountain, taking thousands of pictures. All of the color photographs in this book are the products of Gary's work with the photographers to capture one of the moods or secrets of Camelback.

Driggs' interest in Camelback is not of recent vintage. He was born in Phoenix in 1934 and grew up in the shadow of Camelback. He hiked there as a Boy Scout in the 1940s. He learned rock climbing on Camelback as a member of the legendary Kachinas (A senior Boy Scout group that pioneered rock climbing in Arizona). In 1951, he made the first ascent of the Praying Monk on the northern side of Camelback. It is even more impressive considering the relatively primitive climbing equipment available at the time.

Through the '60s and '70s, he worked with other lovers of our landmark, including Barry Goldwater and his brother, John Driggs, mayor of Phoenix, to preserve its rapidly diminishing public acreage. As CEO of Western Savings & Loan, he played an important role financing numerous developments around Camelback and in shaping others. Those efforts had a significant impact in preserving public access for both hikers and rock climbers.

He has become a virtual encyclopedia of Camelback stories and information. In this book, Gary shares many of these stories, revealing that Camelback is far more than just an impressive landmark.

As we listen to his stories, we find that Camelback is a treasure trove of natural and human history. Some of the most interesting characters that have played a role in the development of the Phoenix area have focused their efforts on and around Camelback. You'll get a slice of Arizona history as seen by the wise, old Camel watching over the Valley. You'll see some of the most beautiful scenery in Arizona and a dazzling array of plants and animals.

The journey upon which you are about to embark is in fact a series of hikes with Gary Driggs.

Initially, through the overture pages, we will encircle our subject from the air. Appraising the metropolis below, its houses and streets flowing up the slopes of our mountain, we are reminded of the reason this Valley has been a major population center for more than 1,700 years—water. The abundant greenery is natural. This city site, located at the confluence of the Salt and Gila rivers, has always been a

The head of Camelback from the northwest. Oil by Ed Mell.

natural agricultural area. The early Hohokam people created sophisticated irrigation canals more than a thousand years ago which still exist today.

And now we hike. Beginning with the Echo Canyon Trail, we will reach the summit from Camelback's north side. Catching our breath, we'll meander over the Camel's Head Trail to Bobby's Rock through Echo Canyon to the Camel's Nose. On the Camel's Tail, the Cholla Trail begins on the eastern slope and wanders past Artist's Point and then follows the ridge to the summit.

The photography shows our routes up the three trails. As we hike, serendipitous stories will unfold about the mountain's history and development. These stories reflect the zeal, enthusiasm, hopes, visions and conflicts between Native Americans and settlers, developers, preservationists and residents.

What a pleasure to share the day—the mountain—and the stories with one who knows them well.

ED MELL

Ed Mell was born in Phoenix in 1942. He received a bachelor of fine arts from the Art Center of Design in Los Angeles and attended Phoenix College. Mell has a distinctive style that he brings to his paintings of Southwestern landscapes. He combines abstraction and realism. Mell says he is drawn to the overwhelming power of desert walls and mountains. He indicates that he has been most influenced by Maynard Dixon and the Taos Ten. Ed says, "The quality that I find important to bring to a piece of art is first and foremost emotion. Then, art needs to bring something different, something that the viewer might not have thought before." Ed Mell has had numerous special exhibits and his paintings are widely held by collectors of Southwestern art.

Gary M. Avey
September 21, 1998

Ode to Camelback

Oh, Gilbraltar of the Valley,
There you stand in mute repose
Against a cloudless skyline
As the evening shadows close.

You're a vivid, stern reminder
That there was a Master Hand
That made you for a purpose
In a waste, once desert land.

But the wisdom of your making
Was for ages lost to man
Until man reclaimed the desert,
Then your usefulness began.

Now you stand a firm protector
O'er a spot like Eden's make,
And "Arcadia" is nesting
There serenely in your wake.

For you to take the chill of winter,
With it cool off summer's heat
And make "Summer's Winter Playground"
All about you, at your feet.

And you've made a barren desert,
From a "Land that God forgot"
To a land of palms and roses,
To a winter garden spot.

And, we're thankful to your Maker
For the hand that put you there—
May you stand a mute example
Of His watchfulness and care.

—The Arizona Republican
December 28, 1924

*View from South Mountain. Photo by
J.R. Norton.* INSET: *McLaughlin
Collection, circa 1930.*

Now to tell our story! Back in 1883 a pioneer in the vigor of life and manhood—a man of faith and hope and courage with ambition for achievement, climbed to the mountain's top on Camelback and gazed across the desert and as his eye traced the river winding thru the plain he realized that water might be diverted over the land and a vision unfolded there before him.

Out of the withered sage and cactus beautiful groves of citrus rise. Fields of green alfalfa lie beyond. Shady drives stretch away for miles between their bordering ash and olive trees. And, lo! A garden neatly tended blooms beside a stream that is to be, and in the garden stands a home.

Inspired by the vision he there resolved to make the dream come true and dedicate his life. . . .

His men and mules dug ditches and turned the water in. Next came the garden—the one beside the stream that was to be—there, almost in the shadow of that desert emblem, image of a recumbent camel carved by Nature's chisels in the sandstone and granite. In the garden among its trees and flowers, the seer of the vision built his home and in memory of his fathers 'cross the sea he called it Ingleside.

—*Ingleside and its Inn*
Circa 1927, Ralph Murphy

View from the south. Photo by Gary Driggs. Aerial services, John Hughes.
INSET: *McLaughlin Collection, circa 1954.*

The Stone Monk

The Praying Monk has
turned to stone.
Kneeling forever—dark—alone
Upon the mountain side
His offered prayers—
Our prayers and his
For centuries
Rise upward toward the Cosmic Tide,
While he prays on alone.

—*Sanger-Stewart.*

View from northwest. Photo by Gary Driggs. Aerial services, John Hughes.
INSET: *McLaughlin Collection, circa 1950.*

Poem From a Guest

Did you ever think you'd like to find
A regular Heaven on Earth?
Some place where you could rest your mind
Near a friendly fireside hearth?

Where you can have an atmosphere
That reminds you of home sweet home;
And yet no worry, or care or strife
Where you are not friendless or alone?

Well, listen, my friend, I've really found
A spot that I know you will love;
A place of beauty, and quiet and peace
With glorious skies above.

Far away from the motley throng
Out on the Desert Land
Nestled beneath Old Camelback
As tho fashioned by God's Divine Hand.

'Tis a spot of beauty and wide renown
Away from all strife and sin,
It's a garden spot . . .'way out in the West;
It's the wonderful JOKAKE INN.

By Zelda Pryor, 1939
—Jokake Inn, By Sylvia Byrnes

View from the southeast. Photo by Gary Driggs. Aerial services, John Hughes. INSET: *McLaughlin Collection, circa 1946.*

On the north side of the Head of Camelback, underneath the Rock Figure climbing the mountain, from a distance is seen an amphitheater arched in the rock: the sun does not penetrate and the rain does not enter; here the untutored mind would discover mysterious echoes . . . Overhead the disintegrating rock is a metamorphosed cyclopean conglomerate, the floor composed of several feet of the fallen, dust-like fragments. For two feet deep the ground is filled with these reeds; searchers have plundered the site, curio-mad, and broken up thousands in quest of fancied trophies. The local tribes loved gaming more than religion, but this hidden shrine was not a gambling house, but rather a church.

—Prehistoric Irrigation
By Omar A. Turney
A.M., M.S., C.E., Ph.D
1929

View from the north. Photo by Bryan Casebolt. INSET: *McLaughlin Collection, 1949.*

ECHO CANYON TRAIL

CHAPTER ONE

ABOVE AND OPPOSITE: *Starting the Echo Canyon Trail. Photos by Bryan Casebolt.*

It's 6 a.m. when I drive into the parking lot of Echo Canyon Park on the northern side of Camelback Mountain for my regular morning hike to the summit. Already, twenty cars line the tiny parking lot. On the winding, sometimes craggy trail above, climbers move in serpentine flow. You can see much of the trail for the first quarter mile. Rocky walls jut almost straight up several hundred feet above the trail. These spectacular rock formations on the head of the Camel are among the most scenic in Arizona.

Camelback Mountain has been a focal point in the Phoenix metropolitan area. It is a place where people have worshiped, dreamed, made and lost fortunes in real estate and other ventures, married and died. This formation is not only beautiful for its elegant and varied shades of Southwestern red, but also for the patina of green and yellow lichens that cover north-facing rocks. The Praying Monk, a 10-story rock monolith, kneels reverently above, giving the mountain a seemingly direct link to the heavens. Homes crowd around the base of the mountain and some crawl up its slopes as people seek higher ground.

The mountain is magnetic, drawing more than 300,000 hikers each year to the summit to gaze out

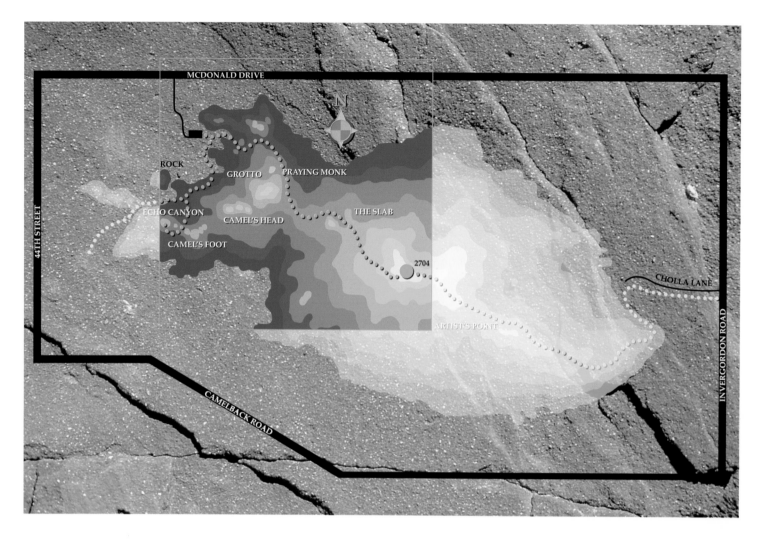

over one of the largest desert cities in the world—a metropolis of more than 2.5 million residents. The metropolitan area covers more land than the city of Los Angeles. In fact, the greater Phoenix urbanized area is so large that several of the world's largest cities, such as New York, Paris and London, would all fit in the space with plenty of room to spare.

Camelback's fabulous rock formations and abundant plant and animal life cover much of the spectrum of geologic features and life in the Sonoran Desert.

Above all, there is the spiritual draw of the mountain. Join me on a journey through time and space up the Echo Canyon Trail, the most prominent of three trails on the mountain.

A SACRED MOUNTAIN

You could spend hours on Camelback and never see a fraction of this natural wonder. But anyone who spends even a brief time on Camelback will find that the mountain will make a lasting impression. That impression will not just be of scenic beauty but a spiritual one, as well. Camelback is sacred space, and has been for more than a millennium.

I don't idly suggest that Camelback is a sacred

mountain. The most authoritative book on the prehistoric Indians and their canals was written by Omar A. Turney in 1929. In that book, Turney noted that a ceremonial cave on the northern side of Camelback was perhaps the most important religious site to have been discovered in central Arizona. He said this hidden shrine was a "church." Since the use of this shrine dates back to the Hohokam Indians or before, I think we can safely say that Camelback Mountain houses the oldest church in the Valley of the Sun.

The Ceremonial Grotto is just south of the Echo Canyon Trail to the summit, near the small ramada located a few hundred feet up the trail. It is a cathedral-sized opening in the rock where some of the earliest peoples, perhaps the Hohokam and their traders from Mesoamerica, stopped to make offerings to their gods using hollow reeds stuffed with herbs or tobacco-like plants. These reeds were wrapped with a finely woven cloth—a sign of their religious nature. These "ceremonial cane cigarettes" were an important part of the religious rites of Native American worship. The ceremonial cigarettes were wrapped in bundles of four or multiples of four. The number four continues even today to have a ritual importance to many

Southwestern Indian tribes.

Today, the mountain remains sacred space. The Roman Catholic Church has two centers for religious retreats on the slopes of Camelback—the Mount Claret Center on the south and the Franciscan Renewal Center on the north. Father McMahon, director of the Mount Claret Center, recently told me that "coming to the mount" has gained meaning for those who have found spiritual renewal on the slopes of Camelback. Father McMahon feels that the beauty and serenity of Camelback has been an important factor in changing lives.

I've seen people meet regularly in a small cave near the trail head for regular scripture reading sessions. Others climb at sunrise to pray. Weddings have been held on Camelback. Many people continue to draw spiritual strength and inspiration from Camelback. Many faiths, including Catholics, Protestants, Jews, Mormons and others have built worship centers near Camelback. In conversations with hundreds of people on Camelback, their spiritual uplift from being on the mountain has been a common theme.

Mountains have long held special significance in many of the world's religions. The gods of surrounding Native populations often live on mountains or are part of a mountain range. In Christianity and Islam, revelations from God often occurred on a mountain: Moses received the Ten Commandments on Mount Sinai. The Temptation of Jesus took place on a mountaintop, as well as the Transfiguration. In some religious traditions, a mountain is the center of the universe, a place for special religious instruction or ceremonies.

Many mountains with religious significance come to mind. A short list of some of the world's sacred mountains include Mount Kailas, Mount Everest, Annapurna and Nanda Devi in Tibet and Nepal; Mount Fuji in Japan; Ayers Rock in Australia; Mount Zion in the Holy Land; Mount Olympus in Greece; Mont Blanc in Europe; Mount Kilimanjaro in Africa; and Denali in Alaska.

In my lifetime of mountaineering I have often climbed mountains that had sacred meaning. I have been touched with a feeling of reverence for the people who gained strength or peace from the power mountains exude. On two occasions I spent more than a month climbing in the Kang Karpo Mountains on the border of China and Tibet. These mountains are among the holiest in Tibetan Buddhism, and a

ABOVE: *Giant saguaro north of Camelback (perhaps the world's largest), McLaughlin Collection, circa 1929.*
BELOW: *A hiker prepares. Photo by Jeff Kida.*

pilgrimage around the mountains gives great merit. Mountains have been important in nearly all religious traditions.

In Arizona, Native peoples hold many peaks sacred, including the San Francisco Peaks, Mount Baldy, Mount Graham and Mount Taylor. These mountains serve as important connections between heaven and earth. Phoenix also has its sacred mountain—Camelback. While most Phoenix residents may not recognize Camelback as a sacred mountain, it has played and continues to play a significant temporal and spiritual role in the life of the urban area.

HOW THE CAMEL CAME TO BE

As we start up Camelback and see the varied shapes, colors and textures of rock, you can't help wondering how this mountain came to be. The remarkable resemblance of the mountain to a kneeling camel makes it a truly whimsical mountain, but the story of its birth and growth is a true wonder.

Geologists tell us that the hump of Camelback is comprised of Precambrian granite nearly 1.5 billion years old. The head of the Camel consists of four layers of sedimentary rock laid down during the past 25 million years. In terms of a comparison, the hump of the Camel approaches the age of the rocks at the bottom of the Grand Canyon and the rocks of the head are younger than the top of the Grand Canyon. Thus, our hike to the top is going to take us through much of the entire geologic history of the world.

The story of Camelback begins about 1.5 billion years ago. At that time, a great batholith of molten rock deep inside the earth was starting to cool into a reddish granite that would later form the Camel's Hump. About 70 million years ago at the end of the Mesozoic era, Arizona was at the edge of the North American Plate, which was colliding with and over-riding the Pacific Plate. The resulting collisions fractured and lifted some of the rocks in southern Arizona. This action was somewhat similar to the impact the Indian subcontinent has today as it crashes into Asia, forming the Himalayan Mountains.

During the infancy of Camelback the area was covered with shallow seas and lots of volcanoes. Volcanic dikes can be seen today, as the mountain gives a vivid reminder of its violent beginnings.

The head of the Camel consists of four layers of sedimentary rock: The Dromedary Member, the Echo Canyon Member, the Papago Member and the Camel's Ear Member. These four distinct layers were

ABOVE: *Lupine on the Echo Canyon Trail. Photo by Jerry Duchscherer.* OPPOSITE: *View to the northwest from the Echo Canyon Trail. Photo by Bryan Casebolt.*

laid down during the past 25 million years or so. At that time, the reign of dinosaurs was long past.

The gap between the age of the Camel's Head and the hump is called in geologic terms an unconformity. The missing layers have been washed into the Salt River Valley. The sediments in the Valley of the Sun reach a depth of several thousand feet. In a sense, the Salt River Valley south of Camelback is a giant lake of sediments laid down over millions of years.

The porous nature of these sedimentary rocks helps explain why such an abundant groundwater supply has been available in the Phoenix area. Until the late 1970s, the water table was declining. But in recent years the water table near Camelback has risen sharply due to reduced farming and a relatively wet period during the last 30 years. Just two miles south of Camelback, in many places, the water table is about 30 feet below the surface. Thus, the Valley below Camelback not only appears to be a great lake of sediments but in reality is also a great lake of groundwater just below the surface of the desert.

The oldest layer of rock on the Camel's Head is the Dromedary Member, which gets its name from Dromedary Drive on the south side of Camelback. The Dromedary Member is most easily seen on the south side where it appears as a pebbly bright-red sandstone 60 to 150 feet thick.

The Echo Canyon Member is the dominant layer at the western end of Camelback Mountain. Two-hundred-foot sheer walls in Echo Canyon dominate this layer. This formation is of granite breccia and metarhyolite breccia. Breccia consists of clusters of different rocks glued together with pressure over millions of years into a single layer of rock—yet the individual rocks still retain their original appearance. This chunky layer stands in sharp contrast to the layers above and below. The individual rocks that comprise the Echo Canyon layer vary greatly in size from very small to several feet in diameter.

The Papago Park Member is the third layer of the Camel's Head. It is named after similar rocks in Papago Park. It consists of tan to red sandstone with numerous embedded rocks and boulders that were laid down in silt and sand beds.

The Praying Monk on the northern side of the mountain, in Echo Canyon Park, is the most prominent element of the Papago Park formation. The Monk kneels on the Echo Canyon layer. From Echo Canyon Park, it is easy to follow the clear line that shows the Echo Canyon layer as it forms the base for the Papago Park layer.

The very top layer of rock on the Camel's Head is the Camel's Ear Member. The Camel's Ear layer is a dark red-brown sandstone. Encased in the sandstone are meta-volcanic rocks (volcanic rock altered by heat and pressure).

The most prominent feature of the head is a giant fault that forms the neck of the head. The present shape of Camelback has been formed during the last 12 million years and those forces continue today, pushing the head up at the fault line that forms part of the trail to the summit.

A STORY OF THE CAMEL'S CREATION

Tall tales have had a long tradition in Arizona. In the 1920s, most tourists came to Arizona via the train. When passengers arrived in Phoenix, one of the popular excursions was the trip to the newly

Echo Canyon Trail and the Ceremonial Grotto. Photo by J.R. Norton.

completed Roosevelt Dam up the scenic but primitive Apache Trail. (Much of the Apache Trail remains unpaved today, and is still a wonderful scenic, but somewhat scary, drive because of the narrow road and steep cliffs.)

One of the premier drivers was Wes Hill, who was a great teller of tall tales. The primitive road and steep dropoffs required a garrulous driver to keep the tourist's mind off impending doom. As Wes Hill drove up the road near the Superstition Mountains, he would call attention to the odd shapes of the rocks, which seemed to resemble various animals. He then told this legend of an early encounter between Spanish explorers and the Pima Indians who lived near the mountains.

Near Weaver's Needle, the Indians led the Spanish explorers to the remains of a huge boat. The Spanish explorers were devout Catholics and were amazed at the sight of a fertile valley. Could this be the biblical Garden of Eden? Could these Indians be the descendants of Adam and Eve? The Indians said that a great flood had left the boat stranded in the Superstitions. When the waters receded the animals left the ark. Those were the animals frozen in stone that Wes had described along the road. In the ark, there had been a huge camel that set off across the desert. But the Great Flood had left the desert floor soft and muddy. As the camel walked across the desert, he became mired in the mud and eventually turned to stone. Thus, the mountain we see today may be a petrified passenger from the great ark.

There you have it—the geologist's version or the Arizona tall tale. For a sacred mountain, anything is possible.

HEADING FOR THE TOP

This morning my friends Gary Edens, Denny Lyon, Sam Linhart and Bill Reilly and I are on a trek towards the summit. I've been hiking this trail for nearly fifty years. But no matter how many times you climb Camelback, it is still an awe-inspiring experience. Over 1.2 miles, the trail rises 1,300 vertical feet to the summit. If we climb steadily without stopping, we'll be on top in a little over thirty minutes. The first few steps take us down into a sandy wash. The bottom is lush with paloverde trees, saguaro cacti and a multitude of shrubs. It is a microcosm of the washes throughout the Sonoran Desert. To our left a striking sandstone formation, pocked with caves, rises perhaps 100 feet over the wash.

ABOVE: *View north from the Ceremonial Grotto. Photo by Jerry Duchscherer.* OPPOSITE: *Ceremonial Grotto. Photo by J.R. Norton.*

We journey up on a series of steps that volunteers built with railroad ties to limit erosion. Eighty steps up, we reach a 30-foot-tall sandstone boulder. Technical climbers call it The Main Boulder. The white dust of chalk marks tiny crevices where climbers practice the sport of bouldering. Bouldering is rock climbing with or without ropes on huge boulders.

A few more steps brings us in the midst of a large field of smaller boulders. Some of the boulders have impressive displays of mosses and lichen resplendent in yellow-orange and several tones of green. When dry the mosses lie dormant, looking more like a black coating than a plant. Pour a few drops of water on them and within seconds the tiny plants turn a bright green. Some sprout micro-sized stems resembling palm fronds. They are perfectly engineered for the desert, maximizing every drop of moisture before blending back into their rocky homes.

This remarkable ability to transform has made lichens, mosses and liverworts among the most amazing plants on Camelback. They tend to grow on the shady or north side of rocks. The lichens, which are a combination of algae and fungus, appear to be a mixture of green, yellow and orange, giving the rocks the appearance of having a crust. They play an important role in breaking up the rocks and creating new soil to sustain the plants on the mountain.

There are several kinds of mosses on Camelback. During the dry periods they simply appear to be a black or brown plant or not even plants at all. Rain converts these mosses to a brilliant display of various shades of green, changing the color and mood of the entire mountain.

My favorite time on Camelback is just after a rain when the mosses come alive. The most widespread is a club moss—selaginella or Resurrection Plant. In its dormant phase this moss has curly, withered brown stems. They appear lifeless. This club moss forms a carpet on much of the northern face of the mountain. It even clings to extensive areas of the nearly vertical walls where water can reach and nourish the plants. The common name is the Resurrection Plant because it comes to life after each rain. Unlike other mosses, which come to life in a matter of seconds, the Resurrection Plant takes a few hours. But, once resurrected, the selaginella is one of the most beautiful plants on Camelback. Depending on the temperature, the selaginella can retain its green color for several days, or even a week or two.

There are one hundred species of plants on Camelback, according to a report made by the former director of the Desert Botanical Garden. These plants include thirty-five separate plant families. I've noticed additional plants not included in that list. That report said, "Camelback represents a veritable island of plants, some of which are not found growing within thirty miles of the mountain."

THE CHANGING CLIMATES OF CAMELBACK

Among the most interesting things about Camelback is how rapidly the environment changes. An entirely different set of plants and animals can be found just a few feet apart depending on whether the area is shaded or in direct sunlight. The steep north-facing cliffs of Echo Canyon and the Camel's Head in particular create a microclimate significantly cooler than the rest of Camelback.

The shaded areas of these cliffs on the northern side of the mountain allow for the growth of desert plant species normally only found thirty miles or more from Phoenix in higher, cooler mountain environments.

These microclimates occur all over the mountain wherever there is a large rock, steep face or canyon, which provide a shaded environment. Thus, Camelback offers in one compact area an opportunity to enjoy a vast array of the beautiful Sonoran Desert plants and animals.

ZONES OF THE SONORAN DESERT

In the Sonoran Desert there are several types of terrains. Many of these can be found on Camelback Mountain. The valleys or alluvial plains are largely covered with a desert pavement that consists of rocks that have been cemented into place with years of erosion. The flats have sparse vegetation consisting primarily of creosote bush and bursage with the paloverde, mesquite and ironwood trees largely concentrating along the banks of the desert washes. The *bajada* is a region of the Sonoran Desert that is often called the cactus zone. The lower slopes of Camelback Mountain are an excellent example of this region with abundant saguaros, barrel cacti, pincushions, and hedge hogs, as well as a dense display of paloverde and other Sonoran Desert plants.

The little canyon on the northern side of the hump of Camelback is a nice example of a desert canyon, albeit a small one. This little jewel of a canyon has the feeling of a riparian area and is full of small water pools, which sustain the animals in the area due to the shade and dense foliage that grows in the small canyon.

The desert mountains are another zone of the Sonoran Desert. The upper slopes of Camelback are an outstanding example of the lower desert mountains. Thus, Camelback affords the hiker or the climber a chance to pass within a few feet from a type of vegetation that is designed to withstand the hottest beating of the desert sun to a leafy set of plants on a northern slope which is covered with a deep blanket of Resurrection Plant.

CHIPMUNK ROCK OR THE MONK'S BIBLE

Just beyond the quarter-mile mark we reach a small saddle in the trail. It gives us our first view of the morning sun and northern Scottsdale. The McDowell Mountains, Four Peaks and the Superstition Mountains line the eastern horizon.

A few feet to the right is Chipmunk Rock. This is a large, rectangular boulder precariously balanced on just one corner. At the base of Chipmunk Rock a

OPPOSITE: *Bringing moss to life. Photos by Jeff Kida.*

Harris Antelope ground squirrel, which coincidentally resembles a chipmunk, darts around, foraging for paloverde and mesquite seeds and other forms of food. From a distance, this rock looks remarkably like a book standing on one corner.

According to one legend, the Monk of Camelback was told never to drop his Bible and was further warned that if he did, he would be turned to stone. Apparently, the Monk did drop his Bible because we do have the stone Monk, and his Bible is still there below. The trail flattens for a couple of hundred yards along a great geologic fault that forms the neck of the Camel. Along the edge of this 300-foot-tall, north-facing wall leafy plants thrive in the shade. In the harsh, almost constant sun on the southern side, such plants cannot exist.

On the left a chain-link fence installed by the city of Phoenix interrupts the natural beauty, keeping hikers away from a wealthy subdivision lapping at the slopes of the mountain. In many ways the fence has become a symbol of the fragile tension between developers and preservationists.

THE U.S. SURVEY OF CAMELBACK LANDS

The land around Camelback was surveyed from 1868 to 1902. The objective was not only to establish the reference points for legal descriptions but also to evaluate the quality of the soil for agricultural purposes and identify all the principal natural features and vegetation. The U.S. survey work was high quality and detailed. The men took their work seriously as evidenced by the oath taken by the chain carriers, George H. Harold and Martyn C. Mowry. In part, they swore in 1898, "We will level the chain over even and uneven ground, and plumb the tally pins, either by sticking or dropping the same; that we will report the true distance to all notable objects, and the true length of all lines that we assist in measuring, to the best of our skill and ability. . . ."

The 1898 survey described the land as "more or less rolling, and sparsely covered by Ironwood, Paloverde, Timber also Saguaros and Chollas."

The first mention of "Camelback Mountain" is in the March 23, 1903, survey. Reference is made to the rolling land along the foot of Camelback Mountain. The text implies the name was in common usage at the time. The soil was described in

OPPOSITE: *Moss and lichen. Photo by J.R. Norton.*

the 1903 survey as "2nd, 3rd, and 4th rate." Farther south by the Arizona Canal the soil was classified "1st rate." In the 1903 survey a company called "The Camelback Oil Company" had erected a derrick and was "going" for oil. There is no record of Camelback Oil's having any success.

The final map of the U.S. Survey of Township 2 North, Range 4, completed between July 1902 and April 1903, gave the mountain its name. HF Robinson is listed as the surveyor. The team sent a flagman to the top of the mountain.

IT'S "CAMELSBACK" IN 1903

When the survey was actually published in 1906 the mountain was called "Camelsback." The 1930 reprint still used "Camelsback." Often, in the '20s and '30s, it was "Camel Back." By 1948 the reprint of the 1906 survey had changed the name to Camelback. In all these editions the summit of Camelback was used as a benchmark at 2,700 feet. We now know the summit is 2,704 feet above sea level, but accuracy within 4 feet is very good for a turn-of-the-century measurement.

VOLUNTEERS BUILD THE TRAIL TO THE TOP

A few hundred feet beyond the Monk's Bible, the trail climbs steeply on steps made with railroad ties that hug the great wall that forms the neck of the Camel. The terrain is steep, so we're grateful for these steps. It's quite a story of how the trail to the summit was built.

After the opening of Echo Canyon Park in 1973, the annual volume of hikes to the summit began to accelerate. There was no clearly defined trail. Rather, a spider web of trails led to the saddle at the one-quarter-mile mark.

A number of Boy Scout groups made efforts to improve the trail. My son, Taylor Driggs, did his Eagle Scout project on Camelback by making trail repairs. One of these Scout projects left some unused railroad ties alongside the trail.

Two new members of the Arizona Mountaineering Club—Paul Diefenderfer and Tim Bombaci—kept noticing the railroad ties and Tim suggested someone should do something. Tim and Paul agreed they would start using the railroad ties to improve the trail by building steps in the soft soil. Paul and Tim did most of the work at first. When Paul was on vacation one year, he received a message from Tim: "I hope it's OK—I just bought fifty railroad ties." On his

ABOVE: *Hiking in the boulders on the Echo Canyon Trail. Photo by J.R. Norton.* OPPOSITE TOP: *Praying Monk. Photo by J.R. Norton.* OPPOSITE BELOW: *Hiking the Echo Canyon Trail. Photo by Bryan Casebolt.*

return Paul found the ties piled in front of his house. Tim had purchased the ties for $2 each from a highway construction site where a freeway was going through a railroad yard.

During the next year Paul, Tim and other members of the Arizona Mountaineering Club would install more than one-hundred steps using the ties. They made a wonderful trail which is much better than the concrete trails installed in other high traffic hiking locations.

The work was back-breaking. Paul designed special packs that allowed two men to carry a railroad tie between them up the mountain. On many of the steeper slopes they cemented Camelback rocks to improve the quality of the trail. Early in the process the city sent a ranger to supervise their work. The ranger arrived in cowboy boots—told them they looked like they knew what they were doing and left.

The trail was developed by this volunteer effort with little cost to the city. Today Paul Diefenderfer runs the Phoenix Climbing Gym, an indoor rock climbing center, and is one of the leaders in develop-

ing climbing skills in the Phoenix area.

When I asked Paul why he was willing to spend so much time building the Camelback Trail, he said simply, "I love Camelback." Paul even had his wedding vows performed on top of the Praying Monk in 1991. Paul Johnson, who was Phoenix mayor at the time, participated.

LUSH GROWTH IN THE SHADE

As we walk along the sheer cliff, the ground is covered with lichen, mosses, leafy plants and succulents that only survive with shade from the direct desert sun. In the spring, this area with its microclimate is so lush that it seems out of place in desert country. This part of Camelback is never touched by the searing afternoon sun.

LOTS OF TALENT ON THE TRAIL

Our group of sixty-something-age men can't help commenting on how fit and attractive so many of the young women who climb Camelback seem to be. Either Camelback does wonderful things for fitness or wonderfully fit people are attracted to Camelback. Whichever is the case, the people climbing Camelback enhance the experience. People on the trail seem particularly friendly. We see Denise, who was homecoming queen at West High in the '50s. She could wear the same gown today.

We run into my sister, Anne Christensen, who usually gets on the mountain even before our early start. She has suffered from back pain most of her life, but climbing Camelback has eliminated the pain. Many other regular Camelback hikers attest to the physical and spiritual uplift from hiking Camelback.

In my own experience, a Camelback climb relieves stress like nothing else. You meet climbers of every age and category imaginable. A significant percentage are visitors from out of town. It's not unusual to see sports teams both amateur and professional using Camelback as a workout.

CAMELBACK INN—"ONLY ONE"

Camelback Inn was among the best resorts in the area. It opened on Dec. 15, 1936. The original developer of Camelback Inn was Jack Stewart, who later remarked, "I had the idea and Mr. [John C.] Lincoln

ABOVE: *Camelback Inn, circa 1940. McLaughlin Collection.*
BELOW: *Camelback, circa 1917. McLaughlin Collection.*
OPPOSITE TOP AND BELOW: *Camelback Inn, circa 1947. McLaughlin Collection.*

had the money." The Inn had accommodations for seventy five guests with rates of $10 to $16 per night for a single bed, and $18 to $25 for a double deluxe, including meals. By the following February after it opened, Camelback Inn was full—an instant success.

Stewart was only 32 when he opened Camelback Inn. He came to Arizona in 1932 as a newspaper reporter for North Dakota's *Fargo Forum*. He had come to Phoenix to report on the infamous Winnie Ruth Judd murder case. Winnie Ruth Judd, a Phoenix nurse, was accused of dismembering bodies and shipping them in trunks, which gave rise to the nickname, "The Trunk Murderess." Stewart stayed on and became the publicity manager for the San Marcos Hotel in Chandler. The following year he became the manger of the Wigwam Inn at Litchfield Park. The Wigwam was owned by Goodyear Tire and Rubber Company and was one of the outstanding resorts in Arizona at the time.

Stewart had the vision of a resort in the desert near Camelback Mountain. He sold the idea to John C. Lincoln, who owned 420 acres at the base of Mummy Mountain, just North of Camelback Mountain. Lincoln put up the land as collateral and added additional cash of nearly $200,000. The site was 12 miles northeast of Phoenix at the end of a dusty dirt road without lights, telephones or water.

JACK THE CONTRACTOR

As an economy measure, Jack Stewart acted as the general contractor for the Inn's construction. Adobe construction would both save money and provide good insulation. They made the adobe bricks on the site, mixing mud and straw. A week in the sun would cure the adobe bricks. After they had completed 15,000 adobe bricks, a giant thunderstorm melted all the adobe bricks back to mud and they had to start over. In spite of the setbacks, Jack managed to open the hotel on time.

Land in the area sold for less than $10 per acre, but in spite of these disadvantages Jack Stewart was dedicated to building a resort that was different from the typical dude ranch. He wanted the design of the inn to reflect the culture of the Southwest. They carved Native American welcome symbols above the main entrance to the hotel.

Lincoln was a risk-taker. He had spent money and made a fortune in other investments, such as the Bagdad Copper Mine. Lincoln also headed the Lincoln Electric Company of Cleveland, Ohio. Stewart had the concept of a desert oasis in which guests could experience the desert through trail rides and social activities. The concept proved to be a big hit with eastern visitors who often returned year after year for their winter vacation.

There were lots of activities for adults and children alike. Jack's wife, Mable Louise Shoemaker, organized such events as the Golddigger's Ball, the Cattle Rustler's Ball and the Madhatter Easter Bonnet contest. The Inn's motto was, "Where time stands still." It was particularly appropriate for the adobe cottages and casual architecture of the Inn, which was designed by a local citrus grower/architect, Edward Loomis Bowes. Stewart's philosophy was, "When you own your own hotel, you can do what you want to do."

There was a big effort to make it a truly western experience. Hop-Along College, the Inn's renowned children's program was named for Hop-Along Cassidy, who repeatedly would take the young visitors at Camelback Inn for a trail ride. In the evenings there were regular square dances for the adults. Jack Stewart not only promoted Camelback Inn but the entire Valley of the Sun. Each year Camelback Inn mailed over one million pieces of literature to travel agencies and prospects around the world promoting both Camelback Inn and desert living in Arizona. Camelback Inn ran frequent national promotions,

and Stewart was one of the most active members of the local business community.

THINGS DIDN'T ALWAYS GO SMOOTHLY

While Camelback Inn was a great success, things didn't always go smoothly. In 1953, the *Scottsdale Progress* reported that Jack Stewart was fined $100 for operating an illegal bingo game at Camelback Inn and his entertainment director, Helen Dublin, was fined $25. However, the bingo fiasco turned out to only be a minor bump in the road for Camelback's progress.

Stewart was a sports enthusiast. He had been captain and quarterback of the North Dakota All State Football Team when he was in high school. When he graduated from college he became the publicity manager for a half-million-dollar stadium drive for his university. In Arizona he continued promoting sports. He was one of the prime movers in bringing Big League baseball spring training to Scottsdale and he was one of five people who guaranteed the bank loan to build the Scottsdale baseball stadium. In 1969 Stewart headed the committee that got the Fiesta Bowl started in Tempe. Stewart was generous in his charitable contributions and was enthusiastic about patriotic activities such as "Christmas Out of the Foxhole," a program he developed consisting of all-expense paid winter vacations at Camelback Inn for military servicemen returning from combat duty in South Vietnam.

In 1967 Camelback Inn was sold to the Marriott Corporation. As Jack would say, "Bill and Allie have been popular guests for several years from Washington, D.C. They have built one of the nation's best hotel and catering companies." Camelback Inn would be the first resort acquired by Marriott. My parents' home was just down the street from Camelback Inn and Bill and Allie had been close friends of my parents for many years. I often talked to the Marriotts when they spent a good part of the winter at Camelback Inn.

Marriott expanded and improved Camelback Inn. They added a golf course and spa to the property, and significantly expanded the number of rooms. Other additions included the $3.5 million Jackrabbit Pool complex.

By 1998 Camelback Inn had 453 rooms. Room rates had risen as well. During the prime winter season rates are in the range of $400 and up. Higher rates do not seem to deter occupancy. Camelback Inn continues to run close to full during the prime winter season. Camelback Mountain continues to be a pow-

ABOVE: *Rock daisies along the Echo Canyon Trail. Photo by Bryan Casebolt.* OPPOSITE: *Rock daisy. Photo by J.R. Norton.* INSET: *Russ Tatum, circa 1930.*

erful magnet for the resorts that cluster around it.

In another interesting connection, Camelback Inn served as the headquarters for Barry Goldwater's 1964 presidential campaign. Today Camelback Inn has a display of Goldwater photography provided by the Arizona Historical Foundation in the Goldwater Gallery just off the lobby.

RUSS TATUM: CAMELBACK LAND PROMOTER

In 1930, Russ F. Tatum offered lots for sale north of Camelback in the Granite Gables development for a price of $630 for a one-quarter-acre tract payable at $17.50 per month for 36 months. Larger lots were also available. The land was promoted as suitable for citrus groves and homes. Several graded roads, including

TOP: *Car show at Mountain Shadows, circa 1960s.*
McLaughlin Collection. ABOVE: *Harris antelope squirrel.*
Photo by Paul Berquist. RIGHT: *Rocks along the trail.*
Photo by Bryan Casebolt.

Tatum Boulevard, offered access. Echo Canyon was shown as the Camelback Conservation District. Tatum was a member of the board of directors of the Echo Canyon Bowl Association, which promoted concerts and activities in Echo Canyon.

Like so many other Camelback developers, Tatum lost his land north of Camelback during the Great Depression.

Today, the Paradise Valley Country Club is located in the heart of the area promoted by Tatum. The well-manicured fairways and greens of the country club golf course are one of the most visible features north of Camelback. The golf course covers well in excess of a hundred acres surrounding Marshmallow Hill, just to the left of Mummy Mountain. My home is on the fourth fairway of that golf course. The view of Camelback from the golf course is one of the most beautiful in the Valley due to the sharp contrast between the green fairways and the varied textures of Camelback. Lots around the Country Club's golf course sell in the range of $750,000 per lot. Tatum had the vision and the right location but his timing was off. His experience has been and will be repeated many times. Russ named the major street through his development after himself, calling it Tatum Boulevard. It remains today as the major north-south road in Paradise Valley. Tatum may have lost his money, but his name is a local household word. But most don't know his first name was Russ.

MOUNTAIN SHADOWS—LUXURY RESORT

In 1959, Del Webb opened Mountain Shadows which joined Camelback Inn as another luxury resort on the north side of the mountain. The resort featured a pool area much larger than any other contemporary resort. While the basic construction of the rooms was not elaborate by current standards, the rooms were large and comfortable and offered a grand view of Camelback.

Camelback has continued to play an important role in my life. My wife, Kay, and I spent our wedding night at Mountain Shadows in 1959. To show the pace of change, our room has been converted to a hair salon because of its proximity to the lobby. Mountain Shadows is now owned by Marriott Corporation, which maintains the property as a top-notch resort.

WE'RE HALFWAY TO THE SUMMIT

A circular trail marker cemented into the ground shows we've climbed five-eighths of a mile. This is

Giant thumb. Camelback rock formation. Photo by Bryan Casebolt.

the halfway point on our hike to the top. We're huffing and puffing, but we know it's great exercise and we're enjoying the workout. A large paloverde trunk in the gully provides a good hold for a welcome lift over a high step. A couple of younger and faster hikers pass us. One girl says she's going for her personal best. We're happy to make it to the top in just over thirty minutes, but the fastest hikers can make it to the top in just over 20 minutes and some have climbed Camelback in less than 20 minutes. Others claim to have made it in as little as 15 or 16 minutes.

ORME LEWIS: LAWYER, CIVIC BENEFACTOR

The first house on the slopes of Camelback after World War II was built in 1947 by Orme Lewis on 13 acres on the north side of Camelback Road near 56th Street. Lewis had purchased 10 acres in 1945 for $350 per acre and later an additional three acres for about $1,000 per acre. The home had three bedrooms and was built of wood frame and white stucco.

In 1949, Lewis formed the law firm of Lewis & Roca, which grew to be one of the largest and most prominent law firms in Arizona. Lewis became one of the most influential civic leaders and philanthropists in the state. He headed many civic organizations and contributed more than 2,000 works of art to the Phoenix Art Museum. He said the art museum was his "church" and he made sure future generations would enjoy the works he spent so much energy collecting.

Lewis was a courtly, soft-spoken man with a quick mind and a forceful personality. I had the pleasure of serving with him on the Maricopa County Courts Commission. He was patient and courteous but kept the work moving to a conclusion. Lewis also had a good sense of humor. He enjoyed telling about an incident with his client, famed architect Frank Lloyd Wright, who pointed to Lewis' house on Camelback and asked, "What's that white barn doing over there?"

At Lewis' request, his ashes were spread on the top of Camelback after his death. I had the privilege of participating in a brief prayer with son Orme Lewis Jr. and his wife, Elizabeth, before we spread the ashes on the top of the Camel's Hump. It is fitting that his spirit looks down from the top of Camelback on the city he loved and help shape.

LAND FOR SALE ON CAMELBACK—CHEAP

Land around Camelback remained incredibly cheap even into the 1940s. In March 1944 Martha Edward Schemer purchased 42 acres fronting on 44th Street just north of Camelback Road for $100 per acre. The acreage included "Motorcycle Hill." She sold the acreage in 1946 for $350 to $500 per acre and threw in the hill for nothing.

While it is difficult now to understand why values would be so low and there would be such little interest in preserving Camelback, it is necessary to recall that growth was very slow in Arizona during the 1930s. World War II did bring military bases and some industries but few believed that Arizona's urban centers would become some of the fastest growing in American history. In 1940 the population in all of Maricopa County was only 168,000. By 1950 it was 333,000 people. The population doubled in the '60s, to more than 650,000. By 1998 the population exceeded 2.5 million people.

Camelback was a popular picnic and horseback riding destination during the 1930s and 1940s. At the time, many citizens of Phoenix thought that the state owned much of Camelback Mountain, and that it therefore would always be available for public enjoyment.

A DEPRESSION-ERA TOUR

During the Great Depression the federal government used every scheme imaginable to create jobs. The agency in charge was the WPA (Work Projects Administration). One of the WPA projects was the "American Guide Series," which produced travel guides for every state. The Arizona guide described in detail a circular tour around Camelback Mountain.

Camelback Road was described as "lined with spacious winter homes and their gardens." The home (now the Royal Palms Hotel) of W.E. Travis, president of Pacific Greyhound Lines, was described as having "a long straight driveway bordered with tall palms. Along the front walls, lining the road, are extraordinary specimens of greasewood and creosote bush that show the decorative possibilities of cultivated native plants."

The Arcadia district was described as "a section of palatial homes on the lower slopes of Camelback, all roads follow natural contours and the native cacti, bushes, and shrubs have been preserved and enhanced by judicious landscaping."

Jokake Inn was described as "a winter resort of modified Spanish-Pueblo type buildings tinted to match the cliffs of Echo Canyon" and "ornamented with indigenous plants."

The distant view of mountains is described as "an ethereal appearance with their many shades of translucent blue and purple." The guide noted that Invergordon Road was unpaved and provided a view of the "PRAYING WOMAN" (now the Praying Monk) on the side of Camelback Mountain. The figure is described as a huge rock resembling "a woman kneeling with bowed head."

When the Writers' Project Guide reached Camelback Inn, it described "Arizona's largest saguaro. It is about fifty feet high and has approximately fifty-six arms." Camelback Inn was simply "a winter resort patronized by wealthy visitors."

At Echo Canyon the reader was urged to shout across the canyon.

THE POST-WAR BOOM CHIPS AT CAMELBACK

By the end of World War II, the rock figure on Camelback's slope was known by almost all as the Praying Monk. That was appropriate because the postwar building boom quickly began to chip away at Camelback and the mountain needed constant

OPPOSITE: *Lichen on Camelback. Photo by J.R. Norton.*

ABOVE: *Chipmunk Rock or the Monk's Bible. Photo by Bryan Casebolt.* OPPOSITE: *The fence marks the line between Echo Canyon Park and Paradise Valley. Photo by J.R. Norton.*

prayers for protection.

Postwar Phoenix was booming. New homes were beginning to lap at the base of Camelback Mountain. Subdivisions began to spread all around Camelback. Grading for subdivision roads began to carve ugly scars on the slopes of the mountain. Aerial photos from the time give these roads the appearance of beginnings of octopus tentacles grasping Camelback in an effort to subdue a prey.

CABLE CAR AND RESTAURANT FOR THE TOP

By 1950, the postwar urge for grandiose projects had reached Camelback. Charles H. Anderson of Phoenix proposed a development on the summit to be reached by a cable car with a capacity of 25 people. *The Arizona Republic* published renderings of the tram showing the station and the train. A base depot was to be located near Camelback Road and 48th Street. The development on the top was to include a swimming pool, guest lodge and restaurant.

Anderson told the newspaper in April 1950, "We visualize it in summer as a spot where many residents will want to go to get up into clearer and cooler air. It would be an all-year attraction. Frankly, it would be along the lines of the Palm Springs Tramway on which $200,000 already has been spent."

CAMELBACK NEEDS TO BE SAVED

Bulldozers, road scars and a restaurant on the top all awakened an awareness that Camelback could be lost to unattractive, haphazard development.

One of the early champions of Camelback was Maricopa County Planning Commission Chairman Casey Abbott. In a 1954 speech, he complained that the state had sold much of Camelback for $150 an acre. The last sale was as late as 1948. His frustration over the failure to save Camelback caused him to quip, "I am interested to know when they are going to sell the Grand Canyon." He said that Camelback was about to be destroyed by "so-called modern progress." Abbott's speech in October 1954 and his criticism of the notion of a restaurant on the top generated an editorial in *The Arizona Republic* that urged protection from those who would "put flashing eyes on the Camel."

The Camelback Improvement Association was incorporated in December 1954 with the stated purpose of the "preservation of Camelback Mountain in its natural state." The primary activity of the association was the submission of petitions to the county Planning and Zoning Commission when proposed developments encroached on Camelback.

LOTS OF TALK, LITTLE ACTION

The bottom line was that there was talk of saving Camelback in the early 1950s but no real action. By 1956 there was a great deal of home building on the slopes of Camelback. The Maricopa County Planning Commission finally took action in August 1956 to limit home development on the mountain to no higher than 1,600 feet above sea level.

Even with this limit, houses could be built all over the head of the Camel. Blasting into the mountain for roads, water tanks and building pads became a regular event. A January 1957 *Arizona Republic* editorial decried the continued development, saying that the Camel had "a busted nose."

Even the Arizona Legislature got into the act by asking Congress in March 1957 to make Camelback Mountain a national monument above the 1,600-foot

Chuparosa in bloom on Camelback. Photo by Bob Rink.

level. These early efforts to "save" Camelback focused almost entirely on the need to preserve an unencumbered view of the mountain above 1,600 feet rather than public use or access. Meantime, the developments and housing kept coming. In an editorial entitled "Progress?" *The Arizona Republic* condemned the creep of houses up the side of Camelback and called their inhabitants "modern cliff dwellers:"

"It does seem a shame to have such a famous natural landmark turned into residential sites for modern cliff dwellers. Those people must be refugees from New York apartment houses overcome by homesickness. But while their homesickness is being cured, the view of the thousands who live in the surrounding area is being spoiled."

The editorial bemoaned that Camelback was looking "more like an old lobster covered with barnacles."

THE 1,600-FOOT LIMIT UNDER ATTACK

More talk took place at a Phoenix Community Council conference in November 1957. The group voted down a resolution to halt development on Camelback above the 1,600-foot level. The group

backed off when attorney Joe Ralston pointed out that since the mountain was privately owned, compensation would need to be paid to property owners if their development rights were restricted.

Thus, the efforts to save Camelback received only words, and even weak words at that, as the 1957 meeting of civic leaders showed. There was no call to action or specific steps taken.

The battle over housing development continued into 1958. In spite of County Planning Policy that restricted building to below the 1,600 foot level, developers continued to push the envelope and attempted to subdivide above the 1,600-foot level.

LADIES' GARDEN CLUBS TO THE RESCUE

As is so often the case, few things really get moving until the women decide. The effort to save Camelback is a quintessential example of this maxim. In 1959, the Valley Garden Clubs formed a conservation division with their first objective to save the scenic values of Camelback Mountain and Echo Canyon. Mrs. C.W. Upchurch, president of the Valley Garden Center, led the group in adopting a policy to establish a fund to

LEFT: *A hummingbird's view of Camelback chuparosa.* RIGHT: *Anna's hummingbird. Photos by J.R. Norton.*

purchase Camelback lands for preservation and push for county zoning laws to preserve outstanding scenic or historical sites such as Camelback.

The women of the garden clubs were clearly leading the charge to save Camelback. Their efforts soon unleashed a torrent of volunteer effort and energy.

The garden club ladies soon had petitions before the county Planning and Zoning Commission urging an acceleration in the effort to save Camelback from further development. One of the ladies, artist Ann Toppel, said, "When I saw the road they had cut in the face of the mountain, it felt like they had slashed me. I almost wept. It just broke my heart."

Mrs. Leon Woolsey was one of the most active in the garden club effort. Her home was at 44th Street and Camelback Road. Mrs. Woolsey valued the mountain and was willing to work hard to see that her view was not impaired.

In April 1959, the women appeared before the County Planning Commission and presented 20 petitions from a variety of organizations including Garden Clubs, Women's Clubs, the Arizona Artists Guild, fish and wildlife groups, American University

Women and the Arizona Parks Board. The primary spokesmen were Mrs. Robert C. Sadler and Mrs. Leon H. Woolsey. Casey Abbott, Planning Commission Chairman, suggested the women approach Senator Barry Goldwater to get his help in making Camelback Mountain a national monument. Mrs. Woolsey said "the Senator had been contacted and he was going to start the ball rolling on that angle." Mrs. Woolsey compared the efforts to save Camelback with the steps taken to save the California Redwoods.

By July 1959 over 2,500 signatures were on petitions to preserve Camelback in its natural state. In presenting the petitions to the Maricopa County Planning Commission, Mrs. Woolsey was quoted in the June 10, 1959, *Arizona Republic* as saying, "Inasmuch as the characteristic silhouette of Camelback Mountain has stood for millions of years it scarcely seems that it should be the privilege of this generation to disfigure and destroy it."

CAMELBACK A NATIONAL MONUMENT?

While committees worked and community lead-

ers filed petitions, developers just kept on building higher and higher on the mountain and the land which could be preserved kept declining.

Even though the unique characteristics of Camelback Mountain exceed those of many national monuments, efforts by Republican John Rhodes to save the top of Camelback met opposition in Washington from none other than Secretary of the Interior Stewart L. Udall, former Arizona congressman. In a letter reported in the Sept. 28, 1962, *Arizona Republic*, Udall said, "Because of the location of this property we believe the local community should be encouraged to preserve the mountain top in some manner for public use."

The Phoenix Gazette retorted on October 3, 1962, "We never thought we'd live to see the day when Secretary of Interior Stewart L. Udall would come out against the central government's acquisition of anything, especially land. But he has. He told the House Interior Committee he thinks the central government should not acquire the top of Camelback Mountain in order to protect it from commercial exploitation."

CAMELBACK'S CHILDREN'S CRUSADE

In the fall of 1963, *Arizona Republic* columnist Don Dedera wrote a column entitled, "This is Camelback's Year of Decision," in which he called on Arizona's children to take up a crusade to save Camelback Mountain from developers.

Teenagers responded with zeal.

Shari Hume, 17, editor of the Arcadia High School newspaper developed the following petition, published in *The Arizona Republic* October 20, 1963:

". . .THEREFORE: Be it resolved that we, the young people of Arizona (less than 21 years old) do respectfully petition the Second Session of the 26th Legislature of the State of Arizona to take appropriate action to permanently preserve Camelback Mountain in its present state for the viewing pleasure of future generations."

The crusade soon spread to other high schools.

TEACHERS SQUASH THE KIDS' PROPOSAL

The objective of the children's crusade was to urge the legislature to pass enabling legislation allowing an exchange of mountain top land for state trust land

ABOVE: *Leafy plants grow in Camelback's shade. Photo by J.R. Norton.* BELOW: *Reg Manning,* Arizona Republic, *October 26, 1965.*

held in trust for schools. The kids were long on enthusiasm but the state's schoolteachers killed the proposal through their lobbying arm, the Arizona Education Association. The teachers' ostensible reason for opposing the exchange was the fact that many state lands were held in trust for Arizona's public schools. It was a somewhat curious opposition because the AEA had not objected to past state leases at very low rates. Nevertheless, the children's crusade gave new life to the grown-ups' efforts to save the mountain. Ed Fitzhugh, editor of the *Gazette*, wrote in February 1964: "NOW THE TEEN-AGERS have shown the way, and one thing seems clear to me: A lot of grown-ups had better put up, which means getting behind the young people to save Camelback, or they had better shut up about how other grown-ups don't provide a good example for the teens."

SLICK ROCK AND RAILINGS

About another fifty steps along the edge of the wall brings us to a level spot about one-hundred feet long. Then, the trail climbs sharply up a slick rock incline. Here, we thank Paul again for a metal railing that he installed on the rock for safety. The fault-line wall overhangs the jagged trail, dwarfing hikers along the base. On the left a steep canyon splits the sandstone layer of the Papago Park Formation, creating a deep canyon with a riparian area at the bottom. The north-facing wall of that canyon is one of the most impressive sights on Camelback. At the top of the railing the trail descends and flattens for a couple of hundred yards before climbing another slick rock area leading to the top of the Camel's Neck. Giant saguaros, paloverde, scorpion weed and a thick carpet of Resurrection plant. A steady stream of hikers of every age snakes along the trail.

A SILVER LINING IN GOLDWATER'S DEFEAT

Indeed, the faltering efforts to preserve part of Camelback received new life in 1964 from two events. One was the decision by the prestigious Valley Beautiful Citizens Council to take on the task of saving Camelback and the other was the defeat of Barry Goldwater in the 1964 presidential campaign.

In November 1964, Valley Beautiful formed the Preservation of Camelback Mountain Foundation and Barry Goldwater accepted the job as chairman.

Having resigned from the senate to run for the presidency, Goldwater was out of work for the first time since he was a schoolboy. He put the full force of his boundless energy to the task. He said, "Saving that mountain has become the most important goal of my life. If it's the last thing we do, we're going to preserve Camelback."—*San Diego Union*, May 22, 1965.

Not only was Arizona's most famous citizen leading the preservation campaign, but he was backed by the most powerful group of business and civic leaders in Phoenix. My father, Douglas Driggs, was part of the group and from his perspective this undertaking had the highest priority.

At the foundation Goldwater was assisted by Mrs. Leslie "Maggie" Kober, who had a great reputation for getting civic tasks accomplished.

Henry R. Luce, publisher of Time-Life and longtime Phoenix resident, also joined the effort. Luce said, "If we can't save Camelback, we might as well disband."

HE PUT HIS MONEY WHERE HIS MOUTH WAS

Goldwater pledged $25,000 of his own money, and his mother pledged another $25,000. He made personal appeals and worked on the project on a daily basis.

He said "This old mountain is worth the fight. A Camelback cluttered with roads and utility poles and bulldozer scars and houses would be the shame of the state." At 57, Goldwater worked with the enthusiasm of youth.

Goldwater used his prestige to convince landowners to either gift or sell land at reasonable prices. One key parcel was a 10-acre chunk of the south face owned by Foxgal Inc. The Galbraith families and Orme Lewis and J. S. Francis, Sr., all helped obtain this key parcel. John Ratcliff committed another key parcel. "Maggie" Kober headed fund-raising. She had served on the city council and was a long time ally of Goldwater. He was the general and she was chief of staff handling the details. The goal of Goldwater's group was to raise $300,000 for land purchases.

By the end of 1965 the campaign was well underway. Newspaper reports indicated the hump of Camelback was safe and the only task was to raise the remainder of the $300,000 needed for acquisition.

Barry Goldwater and Mrs. Kober were a team—going to meeting after meeting to build support for the effort. As Mrs. Kober put it, "We think Camelback Mountain is the most famous landmark in the Valley. It is as significant to some people as the Grand Canyon."

VISUAL PROTECTION—NOT PUBLIC ACCESS

The primary thrust of the Save Camelback Foundation was the acquisition of the land above the

Yes, Virginia, There Is . . .

1,800-foot level to prevent further building high on the slopes of Camelback. Both the foundation and most citizens felt that further scars on the top of the mountain should be prevented.

Most of my own experiences on Camelback had been rock climbing on the Camel's head. I felt it was urgent to preserve a rock-climbing park on Camelback and trail access to the summit. The wealthy residents on Camelback were glad to have the higher slopes protected not only for aesthetic purposes but to keep homes from being built above their own.

In December 1965, I wrote a detailed three-page memo to Goldwater suggesting the inclusion of Echo Canyon in the acquisition program and describing in detail how the zoning could be increased on the 30-acre flat area of Echo Canyon, near McDonald Drive, leaving the rest for public use for mountaineering, picnicking and hiking. I estimated that a cluster-housing plan could provide about 100 housing units in the flat area and still maintain the scenic areas for outdoor recreation.

The memo explained how the park would be closed to night use and, with proper supervision, could allow public use without significant adverse impact on homeowners in the area.

Without such a plan, the public area on the top would essentially be closed to citizen use.

After receiving the memo, Goldwater sent a letter to Maggie Kober asking, "Would you please look over the enclosed proposal by Gary and let me know what you honestly think about it?" I attended a luncheon with Goldwater, Kober and others involved in the effort, but saving the top of Camelback seemed to be the primary goal. Furthermore, Camelback owners wanted development above them stopped, not a public park.

A CAMEL FOR CHRISTMAS

The goal in 1965 was to save the hump of the Camel by Christmas. The effort was given wide publicity by Phoenix newspapers and appeals went out to other cities in Arizona. Barry Goldwater sent a letter on December 7, 1965, appealing for funds. The letter said, "As Chairman, I have contacted property owners and we have commitments to purchase some of this property and receive other parcels as a gift.

ABOVE: *Echo Canyon Trail from above. Photo by Bryan Casebolt.* BELOW: *Reg Manning,* Arizona Republic, *December 1965.*

Now it is up to the citizens of this Valley to raise the money. Our goal is $300,000—a fantastically low figure when you consider the estimated value of this land. We need the help of everyone! A few cannot do it! This is a community-wide effort. . . .We feel it will be a disgrace if the citizens of this Valley allow this effort to fail."

The Arizona Republic, the state's major newspaper, gave the campaign constant coverage. Don Dedera wrote an article entitled "There's Nothing Anywhere in the World Like Our Own Monk and Camel," which reprinted a letter from Howard Seymour, Phoenix Union High School Superintendent, which summarized his family experience in Phoenix. He said, "Highest on any list, however, has always been Camelback and that poor old Monk, always trying, but never quite getting there. The mountain, they all agreed, was the most wonderful background and symbol for a city that they had ever seen."— November 23, 1965.

Money poured in from a wide variety of sources. By the end of November 1965 Goldwater announced half the funds had been raised. Arizona Governor Sam Goddard proclaimed Save Camelback Week in Arizona.

By mid-December, *The Arizona Republic* reported 1,350 individual contributions to Save Camelback.

NO STONE LEFT UNTURNED

The whole community got involved in the effort to save the hump of the Camel. The paper reported: "Cars have been washed for Camelback, cupcakes have been baked for Camelback, citrus has been sold for Camelback, and cans have been collected for Camelback. Treasuries of garden clubs and home rooms and luncheon societies have been raided for Camelback. Margaret Kober has been talking on the telephone for six weeks, and Barry Goldwater has played a trombone while wearing a Beatle wig at a teen-age dance for Camelback."—*Arizona Republic*, December 21, 1965.

By Christmas 1965 about two-thirds of the $300,000 goal had been promised. The smallest donation was 47 cents from a group of schoolchildren and the largest $25,000.

CAMELBACK TAKES FEDERAL MONEY, TOO

In March 1966, the County Parks and Recreation Department filed a request for $200,000 in federal

The first railing. Photo by Bryan Casebolt.

funds to aid in the preservation efforts. The Save Camelback effort started by Mrs. L.N. Woolsey (who lived on the northwest corner of 44th Street and Camelback Road) and the Garden Clubs was finally coming to a successful conclusion. But soon there was another disappointment. The Arizona Outdoor Recreation Coordinating Commission turned down the request because there were no plans to develop recreation use. It was primarily a visual use.

Phoenix went back for federal aid in August 1966 by saying it had an overall plan for recreation and open space. However, the city had not actually planned to develop trails or use of the top of Camelback.

In August of 1967 the city finally secured the backing of the Arizona Outdoor Recreation Commission for a $215,000 grant. The expected cost of 352 acres on the top of Camelback was $555,527. Of that cost $285,802 was from local contributions—largely provided by the Save Camelback campaign. By October 1968 the money was in hand.

LADY BIRD LANDS ON CAMELBACK

At a May 20, 1968, black-tie affair, Lady Bird Johnson presented a check for $211,250—a federal grant to preserve the top of the mountain. Nearly 1,000 political, business and civic leaders attended. After the luncheon Lady Bird asked Bill Shover, public-relations director for *The Arizona Republic*, to hike with her. "Let's walk up this mountain," she said to Shover. She then proceeded to walk about 200 yards up Camelback in her high heels. Photographers followed, snapping pictures of the First Lady in high heels on the rocky trail.

Stewart Udall attended the luncheon on Camelback. Goldwater, who had just announced he was running again for the U.S. Senate, got in his political licks by leaving his seat next to Udall and saying, "This is the first time in my life I ever found myself to the left of a Udall."

Meantime, the City of Phoenix continued to make incremental additions to city land on the hump. In 1969 the city authorized the purchase of 1.5 acres on the northeastern slope and 55.8 acres on the southeastern slope. Another 11.5 acres was added in 1970.

PHOENIX OFFICIALS: CAMELBACK IS SAVED

However, as far as city officials were concerned, the job of saving Camelback was complete. They believed further visual scars on the hump of the Camel would be prevented. Public access to the top had not been a primary concern. Those citizens who did try to climb Camelback were met with objections from the wealthy people whose houses surrounded the mountain. These affluent homeowners welcomed the visual protection of their views of the top but they did not want the general public on "their" mountain.

I had talked to Mayor Milt Graham and other officials about the need for a climbing park in Echo Canyon. The effort to save the top seemed a daunting task in itself and there was no general interest for additional park lands once the top had been saved. All those I talked to at City Hall treated me with courtesy but had no interest in a major effort for trails, climbing and a public-use park.

The city knew about the Echo Canyon property, but a park and trails were not part of the agenda. On December 8, 1969, James Crowley, Acting Real Estate Administrator for Phoenix, wrote to Vernon Pick (owner of the Echo Canyon property) stating that the city wished to acquire the property in Echo Canyon above the 1,800-foot contour level and asking what it would take for the city to acquire the lands above that level.

A NEW ADMINISTRATION

In 1969, my brother John Driggs was asked to run for mayor by the Charter Government Committee to oppose Mayor Milt Graham. Graham had been elected with the support of Charter Government, but he now did not wish to honor the two-term tradition of Charter and retire. Graham had been a good mayor and the job of defeating him looked difficult. But John agreed to run and I agreed to serve as the Charter Government Campaign Manager. In addition to John, there was an entire slate of Charter Government council candidates. This election was to have a profound effect on the further preservation of Camelback.

John Driggs was elected mayor in a squeaker election. The result was decided only after a recount due to errors in tabulating some voting machines.

John Driggs took office in January 1970. The preservation of additional lands on Camelback was not even on the agenda for the Phoenix city government. Since Camelback had already been saved, city of Phoenix mountain preservation efforts had turned to the Phoenix Mountains, which were beginning to feel development pressures just as Camelback had in the two previous decades.

Up the railing at daybreak. Photo by Jeff Kida.

HARD LIFE FOR CAMELBACK RATTLESNAKES

We see a cluster of hikers stopped on the trail just ahead of us. When we reach them, we find a tiger rattler coiled in a crevice near the trail. The snake is motionless, in spite of several onlookers quaking in fear and yet gripped with fascination, observing a deadly reptile in its natural environment. Most residents and visitors alike in Arizona fear the rattlesnake whose bite is at best serious and at worst fatal.

The rattlers fear the people even more, as their diet consists primarily of rodents and people look much too large to generate a snake's interest other than to escape.

The most common rattlesnake on Camelback is the tiger rattlesnake. Their banded color is very similar to the rocks of Camelback, which provide excellent camouflage. The tiger is a cold-blooded animal, which can stand neither the heat of the summer sun nor the cold winter. During the winter most of the rattler's time is spent in the temperate conditions of the underground den. In the summer, most of the hunting is at night when the rodents are out and the hot summer sun can be avoided. The rattler has very poor eyesight and hunts via heat-seeking sensors that allow it to find its prey even in the darkest night. The tigers of Camelback must wait patiently for a rodent to come by. The snake has no ears and can only sense its prey by vibration and by the heat-sensing organ in the pits of its head (hence, the term "pit viper"). Once the rodent comes within striking distance, the snake must hit its target, inject the poison and then follow the heat of the wounded animal so it can complete its meal. The jaws of the snake are detachable, allowing it to swallow a rodent much larger than itself. Down goes dinner, bones and all, which the snake is able to consume courtesy of the powerful juices in its alimentary tract. It's a hard life, with only enough venom for a few shots at any given time and the need for dinner to come to you. The tigers of Camelback have a lot more going against them than for them, so we leave it undisturbed and hope that dinner will come by on a timely basis.

SAGUARO—ENGINEERING MARVEL, HOTEL

The signature plant of the Sonoran Desert is the giant saguaro cactus. These stately plants with almost human-like characteristics can stand as tall as 30 feet or more, with several arms. A mature saguaro on Camelback can weight five or six tons and absorb as much as one ton of water from a storm. A saguaro

ABOVE: *Tiger rattler almost hidden along the Echo Canyon Trail.* BELOW: *Gila woodpecker. Photo by Paul Berquist.* OPPOSITE: *View to the east from the top of the railing. Photo by J.R. Norton.*

has an accordion-like surface, allowing it to expand and contract depending on the amount of water the plant is storing at any particular time. Most of the saguaro is water. As you climb up Camelback and look at the saguaros, imagine that each one is a giant stick of water holding tons of the precious life blood of the desert. The saguaro holds so much water that it can go for many months without new water from a rain. Saguaros can live up to 200 years. However, life starts very slowly for a new saguaro cactus. Thousands of seeds are spread upon the desert by the fruits of the saguaro which mature in June on Camelback. Only a tiny fraction of those seeds will grow into a new saguaro. To survive in most cases the saguaro seed needs the shade and protection of a nurse plant, such as a paloverde or bursage. For the first six or seven years, the new saguaro will only reach a height of 4 or 5 inches. Many of the saguaros literally grow through the paloverde that was the nurse plant that gave the saguaro its initial start in life. As you climb the trail to the summit, watch for the giant saguaros growing up through the paloverde trees that gave them a chance at life. The saguaro does not bloom until it is about 50 years old. At about 75 years, they

ABOVE: *Saguaro growing through its nurse plant. Photo by Bryan Casebolt.* BELOW: *Elf owl in its saguaro home. Photo by Paul Berquist.*

begin to develop arms. The many-armed saguaros on Camelback are well over 100 years old. The saguaro fruits that develop late in June and early July have the shape of an elongated egg. Inside of the fruit is a bright scarlet pulp with tiny black seeds. I have enjoyed many saguaro fruits and they are one of the tastiest foods of the desert. There are lots of desert birds and insects that enjoy this delicacy so there is serious competition for the harvest. The flowers at the tip of the saguaro and each of its arms bloom at night during June and provide one of the most brilliant displays of flowers on Camelback. As you climb Echo Canyon and Cholla trails, you are able to look down from many vantage points and see the flowers from above which is the best way to view the saguaro blossoms. They are an important source of food for the white-winged doves which provide a significant means of pollination for the saguaros.

The engineering of the saguaro is one of nature's greatest accomplishments. This plant, weighing five to seven tons, is able to stand by a system of lateral roots that run just below the surface of the ground for about the same distance as the height of the saguaro. On the rocky slopes of Camelback, these roots intertwine around rocks and give the saguaro a phenomenal structural strength, which allows it to withstand the significant winds that continually hit the saguaro from both desert storms and the other winds that blow across the desert. The center structure of the saguaro is supported by a series of wooden rods forming a circle. These round, wooden sticks that form the skeleton of the saguaro have great structural strength and have been used by Native peoples as one of their strongest building materials. Famous architect Frank Lloyd Wright said that the saguaro was the "skyscraper of the desert," and he drew structural inspiration from it.

The fruit of the saguaro is prized among the Native peoples of the Sonoran Desert. The typical mature saguaro is a literal hotel for the birds that inhabit the Sonoran Desert. The Gila woodpecker drills holes in the saguaros and builds nests inside. The nests maintain quite a comfortable temperature even during the warmest summer days due to the protection from the sun and the natural air-conditioning provided by the saguaro. It is in effect is a great stick of water. Thirty kinds of birds have been observed living in nests in the saguaro. Among these are the cactus wren, elf owl, screech owl, sparrow hawk and starven.

Saguaro in bloom on Camelback. Photo by J.R. Norton.

The saguaros of Camelback are very hardy plants indeed. Some of them can be seen growing on the rock ledges of the head of Camelback and other rocky areas, where it seems unlikely that there could be enough nutrients and moisture to keep the saguaro going. These are tenacious plants with an enormous ability to endure the heat of the desert. As you climb Camelback, one of the games to play, which I have enjoyed, is looking for the improbable places that saguaros seem to grow. On some of the waterfall areas of the head of Camelback, you can see saguaros growing on tiny ledges fed by the occasional water from the falls. They somehow cling to the steep rock walls of the head of Camelback and show their tremendous ability to endure the challenge of desert life on Camelback.

DEVELOPMENT PLANS FOR ECHO CANYON

In the fall of 1970, developer Joe Lort came to my office at Western Savings with a financing request. Lort's company, Western Resources, Inc. of Englewood, Colorado, had an agreement to purchase the 129-acre Vernon J. Pick property in Echo Canyon. Lort, an architect, already had a development plan that called for single-family houses to be spread up to the base of the Camel's head, just below the Praying Monk. This development would have ended forever rock climbing on Camelback and any hope for general public access to the top of Camelback, which had just become public land. For years I had enjoyed rock climbing on Camelback and the thought that climbers would never climb the Praying Monk again gave me a sinking feeling. I told Lort that Western Savings would consider his loan request. My real agenda was to implement the plan I had outlined in the December 1965 memo to Goldwater, in which I advocated a park and trail. For Lort's development, the same number of housing units could be clustered in the 40 acres of relatively flat land on the northwestern corner of the property. My objective was to preserve a technical mountain climbing area in Phoenix and provide public access to Camelback while minimizing the impact on nearby homeowners.

The park would be supervised and only nature hiking and technical climbing activities would be

ABOVE: *The Slab on the northwest slope of the Camel's hump. Photo by J.R. Norton.* BELOW: *Gripping. Photo by Jeff Kida.*

permitted. There would be no night use of the park. Lort planned a guard gate for the community, so the guard could close the gates to the park at night. I knew the homeowners in the area would not support the idea of a park, but Camelback Mountain and Echo Canyon were the most beautiful spots in Phoenix. The public deserved permanent access.

I called John at the mayor's office and told him we had to meet immediately. We both agreed Echo Canyon had to be preserved.

I asked photographer Jerry Duchscherer to go with me to Echo Canyon and take high quality color photos of Echo Canyon for a presentation to the city. I invited Chuck Christensen (head of the Parks Department) to bring several of his staff members for some rock climbing. I brought ropes and we took Chuck and three of his staff up the head wall and around the Praying Monk. I explained how the cluster plan could permit the city to acquire the remaining 90 acres or so for a cheap price but we needed fast action. Phoenix could be one of the few cities in

Scrambling up the Slab. Photo by Jeff Kida.

the world with good rock climbing inside the city. Christensen and his staff members were amazed. None had actually been rock climbing on Camelback. They had not realized how beautiful the area was once you were away from the road and up next to the Praying Monk.

All agreed Echo Canyon would be the jewel of city parks. Every effort should be made to accomplish the acquisition. The area contained the Ceremonial Grotto, so the value was far beyond just the beauty and the rock climbing potential.

Christensen agreed to make it a top priority. He arranged for a quick visit by Parks Board members. The Phoenix Parks Board approved a plan to acquire about 90 acres in December 1970. Once the word from the mayor's office came down that this project had top priority, things moved quickly at City Hall.

Over the next few months a good part of my time was occupied with the effort to save Echo Canyon. I contacted well-known real estate appraiser Walt Winius and asked him to do an appraisal of the land needed for the park. Walt contributed his appraisal work. I secured support from a homeowner's associ-

ation and generated other documentation of plants and animals that would support the need for a park. I worked with other rock climbers to get their formal support. Time was of the essence in order to act before opposition from nearby homeowners, who were furious with the proposal, gained momentum. Many already had sent letters to the mayor's office.

The developer, Lort, also objected, saying that he was concerned about the volume of public traffic that would pass through the residential area on its way to the proposed city lands at Echo Canyon.

However, my brother John had been rock climbing on the head of Camelback. Permanent access to the top of Camelback was such a compelling public benefit that the city bought the land despite the opposition. On December 15, 1970, the City Council approved the plan to acquire 91 acres in Echo Canyon. A limited-use plan was adopted with minimum facilities to discourage long-term public use of the new city lands.

Lort retained about 40 acres of the relatively flat land near McDonald Drive. Houses were clustered just as I had outlined in the 1965 memo to Goldwater. It is a beautiful development and today the homes in Echo Canyon sell at a premium. Lort, however, would lose the development in a subsequent real-estate cycle, just as so many Camelback developers before him had.

Later, Lort worked for the city of Phoenix and is properly proud of both the high-quality development and the role he played in preserving Echo Canyon.

THE SLAB

To the left is a smooth slab of sandstone lying at about a 30-degree angle. It has the appearance of a flow of red, wet sand which has just been solidified. The view of Mummy Mountain and Paradise Valley and the mountains beyond to the north is spectacular. We have the choice of scrambling up the Slab or the main trail, which follows a small gully beginning at the five-eighths-mile mark. There is a large pile of loose boulders near the bottom of the gully. We choose the Slab as it affords a more expansive view.

THE LUCK OF THE DRAW FOR CAMELBACK

Only a few short months had passed since Joe Lort dropped into my office at Western Savings asking to finance a 129-acre development. We were lucky this time. Lort came for financing to one of the few people in Phoenix who would want to turn the

ABOVE: *On the Slab at daybreak. Photo by Jeff Kida.* OPPOSITE: *Looking west to the head of the Camel from the Slab. Photo by Jeff Kida.*

area into a park for climbing and hiking. I had been trying for years to get the city to act on the trail to the top and a rock climbing park. In the 1960s, rock climbing and hiking did not enjoy the general popularity that is the case of the 1990s. The election of John made possible the fast action, since he had experienced rock climbing on Camelback. The fast action allowed the park to be approved before homeowner opposition could be mobilized.

Thus, luck and happenstance played a big role in the acquisition of Echo Canyon Park and public access to Camelback.

Once the park was approved, city staff congratulated itself and said they had intended for years to acquire the area. In fact the city had taken no action until the plan was presented to the city of clustering the houses in one corner and developing the remainder as a nature preserve. At any time since the 1920s when Russ Tatum and others developed the Echo Canyon Bowl Association, the city could have condemned the land for public use and acquired it for a modest sum, but no action was taken.

ALMOST A TRAIL TO THE SUMMIT

Echo Canyon provided the most practical access to the city-owned property at the top of Camelback. The only problem was the need to cross a 25-foot-wide path over the back of several residential lots. Without the easement, access to the top would be impossible due to a rock wall several hundred feet high. The lots were owned by opponents of the park and were located in the Town of Paradise Valley. Cooperation in providing public access from Paradise Valley, with its exclusive one-acre residential zoning, was too much to hope for.

After the City Council approval, John headed to Washington to meet with Interior Secretary Walter Hickle to secure federal aid to assist in the purchase of the Echo Canyon Park. City staff put together a presentation book, which the Mayor took with him. Hickle met with my brother, reviewed the presentation and agreed the proposal had merit and was worthy of a grant. He turned the project over to Assistant Secretary Orme Lewis, Jr.

This was another one of those fortunate events that

ABOVE AND BELOW: *Climbing towards the Cave at the top of the Slab. Photos by Jeff Kida.* OPPOSITE: *Looking out of the Cave at the top of the Slab. Photo by Jeff Kida.*

worked together to make the grant possible. Orme was from Phoenix and had grown up on the slopes of Camelback Mountain. Without his help, the funds may not have been forthcoming. In due time the grant was approved with the condition that Phoenix obtain access for a trail to the top of Camelback.

THE TRAIL TO THE TOP

Phoenix proceeded to file a condemnation action to obtain a 25-foot easement across the back of the residential lots. In January 1972, the Maricopa County Superior Court ruled that the City of Phoenix could not condemn land outside its jurisdiction. In the meantime, on occasion, armed guards had been preventing hikers from going to the top of Camelback. Phoenix offered to build a wall or fence to keep hikers from straying too close to the homes.

Amid this tension, Echo Canyon Park was dedicated by my brother on Saturday, November 17, 1973. I was one of the climbers that climbed the Praying Monk and was in radio contact as part of the

ABOVE: *Looking north from three-quarter-mile point.
Photo by Bryan Casebolt.* OPPOSITE: *The Camel's Head
from above. Photo by Gary Driggs.*

opening ceremonies. It had been almost twenty-two
years since my first ascent of the Praying Monk in
1951. My dream had been fulfilled that Echo Canyon
and the Monk and the rest of the climbing areas of
Camelback would be open to climbers for generations to come. No one at the dedication ceremony in
1973 anticipated the popularity the park would
achieve by 1998.

However, at the time of the dedication, access to
the top was still not available. Hikers still managed
to find their way to the summit via a path that had
been used for decades. Part of the trail to the top
crossed the back of three residential lots in the Town
of Paradise Valley. These lots actually included part

of the great cliff that forms the neck of the Camel.
Thus, it would be impossible to reach the top on the
City of Phoenix property unless a tunnel were
drilled through a few hundred feet of rock.

Eventually, the city had to buy two vacant lots for
a little over $30,000 each and an easement was
obtained over a third lot to create a trail to the summit.
The city provided a fence along the easement, which
prevented climbers from straying onto private land.
The lots turned out to be a real bargain for the city, as
each lot would likely cost about $400,000 today.

ON TO THE SUMMIT

At the top of a gully, above the five-eighths-mile
mark, we get another view of the Valley to the south.
At the three-quarter-mile mark the trail crosses the
ridge of the mountain. To the north a steep canyon
has been carved by an intermittent stream that flows
from the top of Camelback. At its base is another
impressive display of a desert riparian area. From the
three-quarter-mile mark the trail turns right and
climbs into the channel of the stream, lined with
abundant desert plants. Occasional flowers are found
in this shaded area even during the hottest months of
the summer.

By the seven-eighths-mile mark we are now at
about the same elevation as the top of the head of the
Camel. Saguaro cacti flourish here, some towering 30
feet high. The saguaros, engineered to draw up tons
of water into their vertical trunks, are literally burst-
ing at the seams from abundant spring rains.

From the three-quarter-mile mark to the one-mile
mark, hikers scramble up one of the steepest, most-
bouldered sections of the mountain. Rock daisies
grow among the rocks, offering a vivid but tiny
accent of color. The final few hundred feet to the
summit affords a spectacular display of lichen-cov-
ered rocks and desert foliage.

Hikers are almost always friendly on the trail,
encouraging each other along the way. They are like
pilgrims on a journey, seeking their own forms of
solace, spirituality, mental and physical health and
respite from the metropolis below. The diversity of
the Camelback climbers is truly amazing.

As you climb the mountain regularly, faces and
bodies become familiar, even at a distance.
Camelback climbers range from young children with
their parents to senior citizens in their 70s and 80s.
Camelback is not just a magnet for locals. A significant ratio of the climbers are visitors from around the

nation and the world. A camera usually identifies the tourist. We stop to greet one such couple, as if we already knew them.

At 2,704 feet above sea level, the summit provides a marvelous panoramic view of the Valley. No matter how many times you climb Camelback there is always a sense of accomplishment when you reach the summit.

The summit is on the edge of a 200-foot vertical granite wall on the northeastern side of the Camel's Hump. The wall is home to a large colony of swallows. In the morning they dart furiously around the top before disappearing into tiny cracks in the north-facing wall. They have chosen the north face for its almost constant shade, which makes for a cool home even during the blistering hot summer.

With more than 2.5 million residents, the Phoenix metropolitan area is one of the largest desert cities in the world. The city truly looks like an oasis from the top of Camelback. Countless trees and several hundred thousand acres of farmland blanket the flatlands below. In just a little more than a century, this mountain has witnessed some of the most spectacular urban growth in North America.

World War II brought most residential development to a halt, but air bases and defense plants brought a new economy to the Valley and thousands of servicemen passed through the Phoenix area. Many would return after the war to help fuel the post-war boom in Arizona. The visiting GIs were attracted to Camelback but not always with a favorable result. In early April 1946, *The Phoenix Gazette*'s Kenneth Arline reported that two sheriff's deputies, recently discharged from the Army, where they received training in mountain climbing, found practical use for their wartime experiences by rescuing an 18-year-old merchant marine from one of Camelback's ledges. The merchant marine, Truman Oliver, had gone up the mountain to take some pictures late in the day and "got caught by darkness," according to the news account.

Oliver would be one of many climbers drawn up the mountain, for better or worse, during the latter half of this century.

STAR POWER AND THE TENNIS RANCH

Looking north from the summit, one of the prominent features below are the tennis courts of Gardiner's Resort on Camelback. The story of the evolution of this resort is another colorful chapter in Camelback's history.

The Paradise Valley Racquet Club opened for business in 1956 with lots of fanfare and publicity. This latest Camelback development had both location and star power going for it. The owners were Hollywood actors John Ireland and Joanne Dru. But the club only had courts and a clubhouse. The Club was a financial failure. After a series of bankruptcies and financial problems, the Club was acquired in 1967 by a group headed by John Gardiner, who had operated a tennis ranch in California for ten years.

Gardiner's plan was to convert the Racquet Club into a tennis resort. That posed a challenge because the club and much of the north side of Camelback were now part of the Town of Paradise Valley.

Paradise Valley had been incorporated in 1961 with the single objective of preserving one-house-to-the-acre zoning. The Town of Paradise Valley didn't want commercial development. However, Mayor Jack Huntress was a practical man and realized the club would continue to fail without a hotel component. The town and Gardiner worked out a deal that would allow Gardiner to add 41 casitas, 12 homes, and four more tennis courts clustered close to the clubhouse. The club's 54 acres was one of the larger parcels on the mountain. Its development would have a major impact on Camelback.

Gardiner asked Jerome Diethelm and John Jakob from the Arizona State University School of Architecture to develop plans for the new resort. Gardiner hired a full-time landscaper. A major effort was made to make the tennis ranch compatible with Camelback. The tennis courts are now obscured by a huge oleander hedge on McDonald Drive.

Gardiner opened the new tennis ranch in January 1970. Casitas were offered at $57,000, but purchasers could only use their casitas for brief periods twice a year. John Gardiner's Tennis Ranch, like other Camelback resorts, has attracted its share of the rich and famous. Pop singer/songwriter Elton John has been a guest. He brought his own cook in order to avoid eating in the resort's dining room. Katherine Hepburn stayed but didn't use the tennis courts. Other notable guests have included Pete Rozelle, Andy Williams, Merv Griffin, Eva Gabor, Bil Keane, Arthur Murray and Clint Eastwood.

John Gardiner's Tennis Ranch has now changed

OPPOSITE: *Golden-eye (above). Photo by J.R. Norton. John Gardiner's Tennis Ranch (below), 1979. Photo Landiscor.*

its name to John Gardiner's Resort on Camelback. Many wealthy people continue to vacation there. However, the current activities at the resort are dull when compared to the early days of the Paradise Valley Racquet Club, when the friends of Ireland and Dru regularly visited the club. In those days there was no hotel but there was one bungalow that served as a private hideaway for many of the most famous Hollywood celebrities of the 1950s. Local Phoenix teenagers worked at the club as busboys, dishwashers and manual laborers. Now grown but still around, some remember Jeff Chandler and Esther Williams, who were frequently seen meeting at the bungalow. Numerous other movie stars of the '50s, including Dean Martin, were seen with various women at the bungalow. What went on inside the bungalow will never be known, but the sight of the Hollywood personalities at the club created lots of fodder for internal gossip among the staff.

If only rocks could talk . . .

FROM ROMANCE TO THE ROYAL PALMS

Looking to the south from the top of Camelback we see the dense date palms of the Royal Palms Hotel, with a subdivision of new houses being built just to the right. The Royal Palms is one of the most luxurious hotels in Phoenix and its history has a lot of strange twists and turns.

In 1927, Delos Cooke built a winter home on 40 picturesque acres on the south slopes of the head of Camelback. Cooke was a well-known New York corporate official and his plans to build were reported with a picture of the home on the front page of the January 30, 1927, *Arizona Republic* with this headline: "New York Man to Build Beautiful Winter Home."

And beautiful it was. It was reported that Cooke spent upwards of $1 million building and furnishing the estate. There were nine hundred date palms on the property and an extensive cactus garden. Rare 15th-Century Spanish furniture filled the fifteen-room mansion.

Cooke had been a vice-president of the Erie Railroad at the beginning of World War I. He was called to Washington to take charge of Red Cross transportation in Europe. He also worked for the governments of England, France and Italy. Both Italy and France gave him their highest honors.

After World War I, Cooke became a director of the Cunard Lines, Baltimore and Ohio Railroad, Chrysler, Foreman State Bank of Chicago and others.

Even though Cooke was a famous executive and could have had many important corporate positions, he was a true romantic with a deep commitment to his wife. About the time he built the Camelback mansion Cooke told *The Arizona Republic*, "My wife's health having been delicate for some years, and my principal object in life having always been to give her every possible help and comfort. I resigned all my official duties so that Mrs. Cooke and I might enjoy our remaining years together." A good part of those last years were spent next to Camelback Mountain.

BIGWIGS FOLLOW IN COOKE'S FOOTSTEPS

After Cooke's death in 1931, the estate was sold to W.E. Travis, President of Greyhound Bus Lines. It was later sold to John J. Ross, President of the Aviola Radio Company.

FROM COOKE TO THE ROYAL PALMS

After World War II, A. Stovall, Fred M. Jahn and Leonard C. Schwenke acquired the Cooke estate and remodeled it as the Royal Palms, a deluxe resort. The new owners of the Royal Palms spent $2 million to convert the estate to a resort, with rooms opening at $35 a night. One of the touches added by Stovall was a collection of 300-year-old tile. The tiles had been shipped by the King of Spain to the new world for a Roman Catholic mission, which was never built.

During the 1980s the Royal Palms fell into disrepair. In 1994 the Royal Palms was purchased by Fred Unger for $5 million. A planned $2-million refurbishing turned into $25 million. Thus, the Royal Palms in 1998 exceeded its former glory. It has, however, been reduced in size and most of the palm trees have been cut down and its golf course converted to a subdivision of expensive homes. Rooms at the Royal Palms now go for $300 and up during the winter season, a far cry from the post-WWII rates.

THE VIEW FROM THE TOP

At the top we chat with a couple visiting Phoenix from Chicago. We offer to identify the mountains we see. Forty miles directly to the east is the jagged profile of the Superstition Mountains, home of the fabled Lost Dutchman Gold Mine. The mine has never been found but many people have died looking for it. The low mountains in front of the Superstitions are the Goldfield Mountains. Gold was

OPPOSITE: *Camelback's summit. Photo by Gary Driggs.*

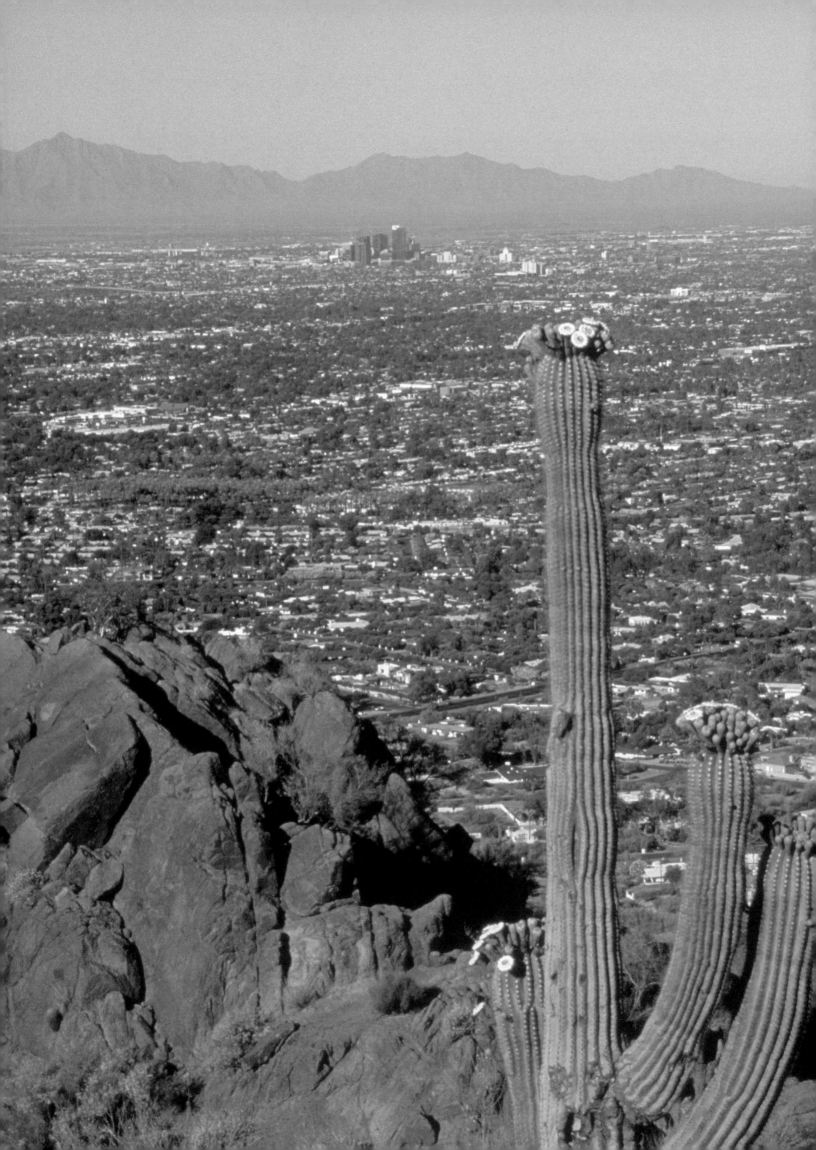

found there and the town of Goldfield is now a tourist attraction. Just to the north of the Superstitions are Four Peaks which are the highest mountains in view at 7,500 feet. They are covered with a pine forest and are capped with snow several times each winter.

In front of Four Peaks are the McDowell Mountains about fifteen miles to the northeast. There is an effort to make much of the McDowells a park but the most important rock climbing area around Tom's Thumb has not been preserved. Thompson Peak with the towers on top is over 4,000 feet high. To the north, we see Pinnacle Peak. Just beyond we see Black Mountain, which is in both Carefree and Cave Creek, and marks the northern edge of Paradise Valley. Beyond is Tonto National Forest.

The mountains just north of Carefreee have colorful names such as Skunk Ridge and Skull Mesa. Lots of gold came out of the mountains north of Cave Creek. The big mountains to the northwest are the Bradshaws, which used to have a city campground in the pines to give citizens a close by cooling off spot at Horse Thief Basin.

The low mountains in front of the Bradshaws are the Hieroglyphic Mountains—none there, but there are petroglyphs. Directly to the west are the White Tank Mountains thirty miles away. To the southwest the big mountains are the Sierra Estrellas some thirty miles away. South Mountain Park, directly south, is the largest municipal park in the world. To the southeast are the San Tan Mountains, another county park.

POPULARITY OF THE ECHO CANYON TRAIL

The Echo Canyon trail to the summit of Camelback Mountain is not only one of the most popular hikes in America but arguably the most beautiful short mountain trail in the country.

Why is this so? Explaining the beauty and magnetism of nature is always difficult but you know it when you see it. Some elements are clear. The Echo Canyon trail offers both spectacular rock walls and interesting geologic formations seldom seen on a single mountain. The trail offers a vast array of different plants and animals. Add to this a rich archaeological and modern human history and you have a spectacular climb.

ABOVE: *The top of Camelback. Photo by J.R. Norton.*
BELOW (L TO R): *Bill Reilly, Gary Edens, Denny Lyon, Sam Linhart, Gary Driggs. Photo by Bryan Casebolt.*
OPPOSITE: *Downtown Phoenix. Photo by J.R. Norton.*

CAMEL'S HEAD TRAIL

CHAPTER TWO

ABOVE: *The Ceremonial Grotto. Photo by Bryan Casebolt.* OPPOSITE: *Giant boulders in Echo Canyon. Photo by J.R. Norton.*

From the Echo Canyon Park parking lot about twenty steps down the trail brings us to the bottom of a dry wash. The trail marker at the wash gives us the choice of the trail to the summit or another to Bobby's Rock.

This morning our group will take the Bobby's Rock alternative. The bottom of the wash is full of sand and rough gravel—evidence of significant past water flows. But today the wash is bone dry.

GROTTO—CENTER OF ANCIENT RITES

As we look at the huge vertical walls of the head in front of us, the most prominent feature is the cavernous Ceremonial Grotto at the base of the cliffs. We walk to the base of the cliff and into the grotto. Once inside the grotto, we find it much larger than we anticipated—the ceiling soars about 50 feet above us. The top of the grotto forms an almost perfect arc that gives the feeling of a natural medieval cathedral.

Dr. Omar Turney, F.R.G.S., surveyed ancient Hohokam canals in 1922, and noted the Grotto in his maps of the area. Like others before him, Turney found cane reeds that had been decorated with a woven material and filled with an herb and possibly

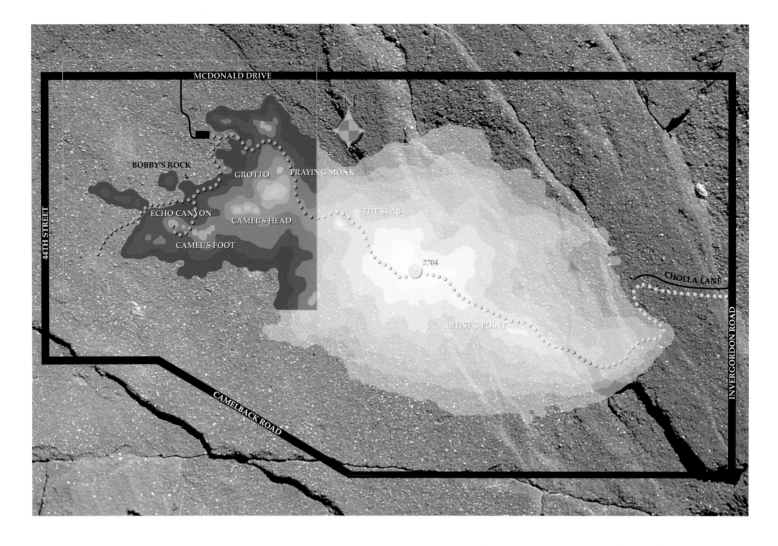

smoked during a ceremony.

Turney understood the importance of Camelback as a religious site. In 1929, he wrote: ". . . From a distance is seen an amphitheater arched in the rock: the sun does not penetrate and the rain does not enter; here the untutored mind would discover mysterious echoes; here a few could hold the fastness against a tribe. . . . The local tribes loved gaming more than religion, but this hidden shrine was not a gambling house, but rather a church. These reeds belong to no archaic rites of departed races; they are mentioned for the reason of the persistent story of their great antiquity." Nearly two decades earlier, in 1911, a local newspaper article is the first written record I found noting Native American interaction with Camelback Mountain. The news story said that Phoenix merchant H.A. Diehl, while on a fall picnic with family and friends, had discovered "several pieces of cane from two to three inches long and varying in size

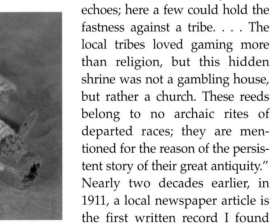

from that of a lead pencil to a half inch in diameter."

On Christmas Day that year, Diehl and friends dug into the floor of the grotto and found more cane, several turquoise beads, obsidian arrowheads, pieces of stone axes and "a number of small bones that might or might not be part of the human frame." Will Lowe, who was a member of the expedition, also found a string of six beads.

Many of the cane pieces were wrapped with a coarsely woven cloth. When the cloth was unwrapped, the fabric revealed what seemed to be either a double cross or a representation of a human figure, marked in black ink.

"Another thing noticed about the canes is that each of them is filled with the seeds or fiber of some plant or plants, giving them the appearance of hard-shelled cigarettes," the news article noted. One piece of cane, a half of a split section, is also marked as though with ink, with a number of x's.

Sharlot Hall, a territorial historian at the time, said she had heard of similar discoveries of reeds or canes on the upper Verde River north of Phoenix.

F.E. Cooley, an employee of Diehl, sent samples of the canes to the Smithsonian Institution in

Washington and received a reply saying that the canes were probably used in a ceremony and that the grotto was a shrine. The canes were "offerings to the Gods," stated a letter from the Smithsonian, "a sort of incense to the Gods and the cloth or fiber placed on the outside representing an article of worth, sometimes represented by shell beads, which were to a certain extent Indian currency. In other words, they purchased the favor of the God and flattered them with incense." The Smithsonian then offered to keep these "sacred cigarettes," since it had only one or two similar specimens in its collections.

In 1959, an Arizona State University archaeology class , led by Dr. Michael J. Harner, excavated the ceremonial cave. Students only partially excavated the site, but their findings confirmed that the cave was used for religious purposes. *The Arizona Republic* reported the class findings in a June 3, 1959, article. In part, the article stated, "Testifying to the actual use of the natural cavity were bundle upon bundle of centuries-old cigarettes, often found with solid pieces of salt. Each bundle was of four, or multiples of four, a number which is, even today, a ritual number in many Southwestern Indian tribes."

Shell beads, presumably traded from Southern California coastal tribes, and fragments of cane, incised and painted in the incisions, were among the articles dug from the deep dust. The latter may have been used in a sort of dice game, according to Harner, who estimated that the objects were placed in the grotto sometime after the year 1200.

Other archaeologists, including the famed Emil W. Haury, who excavated Snaketown and other prominent Hohokam sites south of Phoenix, also noted that the "ceremonial cigarettes" were evidence of ritual use of the grotto by the Hohokam and their descendants.

Camelback Cave, or the Ceremonial Grotto as Turney called it, does have a feeling of serenity and spirituality. I often go to the cave, and its one of my favorite stops for out-of-town guests. They inevitably share my feelings of awe at being in an ancient natural church.

Camelback is a sacred mountain. It is the oldest church in the Salt River Valley. It deserves the reverence and respect as a true sacred mountain. Anyone

RIGHT: *A dry Cudia City Wash. Photo by Bryan Casebolt.* OPPOSITE PAGE INSET: *Cane cigarettes, photo courtesy of Arizona State University.*

who visits the ceremonial grotto will be touched by the spirit of Camelback.

DROUGHT AND DELUGE

The area around Camelback receives about seven inches of rain a year, coming in two very different rainy seasons. The winter rains come primarily during December through February and are usually soft, continuous rains from storms originating in the Pacific and following the jet stream across the continent. About half of Camelback's rain comes during the summer "monsoon" season from July through September.

Arizona's monsoon is a junior version of the same weather phenomenon that affects the Indian subcontinent and the Himalayan Mountains. The monsoon arrives as super-heated air rises from the Arizona desert, drawing in moist air from the Gulf of California and the Gulf of Mexico to the south. "Monsoon" is derived from the Arabic mausim, meaning "season" or "wind shift." Arizona's monsoon is indeed a wind shift because the winds then come from the south and southeast, as compared with the usual from west to east across the state. As the moist air hits the mountains, huge thunder-

Clouds over Camelback. Photo by J.R. Norton. INSET: *Waterfalls on Camelback. Photo by John Driggs.*

clouds form. Dust stirred up by the wind shift blows into the clouds and forms nature's host for the moisture, which attaches to the tiny dust particles and, as their weight increases, fall as rain.

Not only does Arizona's monsoon bring impres-

sive cloud formations, rain and dust storms, but the summer displays of lightning around Camelback are truly one of nature's wonders. An Arizona monsoon thundershower can drop several inches of rain in less than an hour.

During a monsoon storm, Camelback changes from an arid desert mountain to a water wonderland. Dozens of waterfalls cascade from the steep cliffs of the head of the Camel. The washes, like the one we're standing in, become torrents of raging water. Visitors to Arizona wonder about road signs at wash crossings that read, "Do Not Cross When Flooded." Arizona is the only place I know of where water flowing within the identified banks of a river is called a "flood." Water just doesn't seem to be normal in these parts of the Sonoran Desert. That's because most of the year the rivers, streams and washes here are bone dry.

And yet, this dry stream bed is thick with young paloverde, creosote bushes, a million insects, grasses, tiny flowers, even mosses—evidence of the nourishing effects of water and the almost miraculous ability of the desert to make the most of this rare resource. Life is everywhere along the edges of the desert wash, which also serves as an animal freeway.

Evidence of the "floods" that race through these beds also is abundant—testament of the destructive power of water, as well. During one of these storms washes, arroyos and streams quickly fill with a surging stream of water, which sends sand and boulders cascading down the mountain. Just as quickly as the thunderstorm arrives—a half hour or less—the storm is gone and the water has washed into the desert washes. We call it a flash flood. Downstream, rocks the size of a small car are piled on top of each other. In the 1950s and 1960s, the rusted hulk of a car was embedded in this dry wash for years until someone, or some flood, yanked it out.

Waters from the north side of Camelback drain into the Cudia City Wash, which empties into the Arizona Canal just beyond 40th Street near Camelback Road. Each year several people are killed or injured by desert flash floods in Arizona. It is hard to imagine how fast the desert floods come and go. The Cudia City wash, has claimed its share of victims. As evidence of the immense power of the water flow from Camelback, some friends of mine were nearly killed and their car destroyed when they

Storm on Camelback. Photo by Gail Driggs.

attempted to drive across the Cudia City Wash west of Camelback during a summer storm.

ON TO BOBBY'S ROCK

From the wash, we climb up and down about ninety steps made from railroad ties that go along the fence of Joe Lort's subdivision to the right. On the left, is a small, handsome rock pinnacle that rises about 60 feet. The lower rocks of the Pinnacle are the Echo Canyon Formation and show clearly how it is made up of individual rocks that have been pressed into a single layer. The north side of the pinnacle is covered with beautiful yellow lichen. Beyond the pinnacle, we get a great view of the Praying Monk above us.

A MONK BY ANY OTHER NAME

The Praying Monk on the north slopes of the head of Camelback is a familiar landmark in the Valley. But as we have seen in the WPA Writers' Project of the 1930s, it has not always been the Praying Monk. Just after the turn of the century, in the early 1900s, the stone figure on the mountain was usually called "The Old Man" or "The Old Man of the Mountain." In the Writer's Project, the Arizona guide, it was the "Praying Woman." In the 1920s, the Ceremonial Grotto in Echo Canyon was described as being underneath the "rock figure climbing the mountain." In W.L. Lively's 1928 poem about Camelback, "The Legend of Camelback," it was an Indian chief turned to stone. It's also been a "Kneeling Monk" and now a "Praying Monk." It's a good reminder that few things in life remain constant, not even rocks on a mountain.

A REAL CLIFFHANGER

As we leave the Ceremonial Grotto, the trail follows along the edge of the sheer north-facing walls of the Camel's head. The steep, rocky cliffs of the head now rise 300 feet above us and provide almost constant shade for a band of leafy plants at the base of the cliffs. The looming wall above us is called Suicide, so named by Bob Owens, who made the first ascent in 1948. My first ascent of Suicide was with Bob in 1951 and I believe his description of the wall is apt. There is a large rock with a white spot and a clump of foliage in the middle of Suicide. At the base of Suicide is a dense growth of leafy plants since the area is almost always in shade. About 500 feet fur-

Waterfalls on Camelback. Photo by John Driggs.

Flowing streams on Camelback. Photo by J.R. Norton.

ther on the trail from Suicide we come onto the huge bowl that forms Echo Canyon. Bobby's Rock, a separate rock cube about 100 feet high, sits to the right, and to the left is a smooth rock face that gives the best echoes in Echo Canyon. On the top of the ridge to the left we see the Camel's foot. This red rock looks like an upside-down camel's hoof. The high-rise buildings of central Phoenix peek through a pass further down the trail in front of us.

A DETOUR TO THE TOP OF ECHO CANYON

A narrow trail to the left is marked by a series of silver scrolls painted on the rock to resemble ancient petroglyphs. These tiny trail markers are spaced at about fifty feet along the path that leads to Boulder Canyon and the top of the smooth, sheer rock that is the most prominent feature of Echo Canyon. We continue for about 500 feet into the large sandstone rocks in Boulder Canyon. The canyon ends in a steep face called the Yellow Wall by rock climbers. I've climbed it many times—once at night in a rainstorm to rescue a couple of kids that were trapped on top of the mountain. The silver scroll trailmarkers continue up

a rock face for about 60 feet that requires both hands and feet to climb it. The trail continues for a few hundred feet to the top of the Echo Canyon Rock. This is a secret summit on Camelback unknown to most hikers. To the north we look straight up Tatum Boulevard. To the west and south Phoenix spreads out below us. This viewpoint is not as spectacular as the top of the hump, which blocks our view to the east, but it is close. The advantage of this summit is that there is virtually never anyone else on the trail. As we descend we take another short detour to the Camel's foot for more impressive views of the Valley and the south side of the Camel's head.

A PEEK AT THE SOUTH AND DOWNTOWN

We can see much of the urbanized area of Phoenix. South Mountain is relatively low and flat but does form a clear southern border for the city. The more distant Estrella Mountains to the southwest rise a couple of thousand feet above South Mountain and provide a beautiful frame for the picture of the Valley, with a series of graceful peaks. To the southeast, Picacho Peak can barely be seen. The

ABOVE: *Camelback runoff. Photo by Bryan Casebolt.* BELOW: *Copenhaver Castle. Photo by J.R. Norton.* OPPOSITE: *Waterfall on the north side of Camelback. Photo by J.R. Norton.*

high-rise buildings of downtown and Central Avenue tell us at a glance that Phoenix is now a major business center. What is most impressive is how green the urban area seems to be. The trees are so dense that it looks like Phoenix has been built in a forest. Just below us to the east we see a road going to the Whitman house, with its surrounding oasis.

FIRST HOME HIGH IN THE MOUNTAIN

In 1949, Joe Whitman built the first home high on the south side of the mountain. He built a steep hillside road to reach the site, which was behind a natural spur in the south slopes of the hump. The site was planted with palm trees and created the feeling of a desert oasis. I spent time in the home in 1951 with Joe's stepson Dave Sowles, a mountaineering friend. It was the only house, high on the mountain at that time. Joe Whitman's father had founded the town of Whitman, Arizona.

They developed a custom of hanging lights below their home that spell out "Merry Christmas" and after Christmas, "Happy New Year." Those words

can be seen from miles away and have become a major holiday tradition for Phoenix. The current owners of the home, Mr. & Mrs. Jim Warne, still maintain the Christmas greeting tradition.

A MEDIEVAL CASTLE ON CAMELBACK?

Just below us, is a home that has the appearance of a medieval castle. This modern-day keep towers above all of the other houses on the slope and has the feeling of some lord's fortress looming over his serfs below. How did a castle get on Camelback?

A few of the animals of Camelback. UPPER LEFT: *Raccoon.* UPPER RIGHT: *Harris hawk.* MIDDLE LEFT: *Gila monster.* MIDDLE RIGHT: *Coyote.* BELOW: *Great horned owl.* *Photos by Paul Berquist.*

The 8,000-square-foot castle with eight levels and seventeen rooms is the handiwork and dream of Phoenix dentist Mort Copenhaver. In 1966 he acquired two acres on the southern side of the Camel's Head and started building his dream castle with rocks he carved by hand out of Camelback Mountain. It is said that the uniform size of the rocks is the result of Copenhaver wanting to keep each rock under one hundred pounds so that he could carry them to the construction site. Just building a 350-foot road to the building site was a daunting task. The first year he progressed 18 inches. Copenhaver did much of the work on the castle himself, often sleeping only two or three hours a day. He laid each stone himself without machinery.

When Copenhaver needed extra help, he either bartered for it or hired inexpensive Mexican laborers. Once his bulldozer exploded and put him in the hospital for a month with burns. Copenhaver's records show he used thousands of bags of cement. He had an eye for salvage. Iron balconies came from the old Fox Theater in Phoenix and wood for doors from the Santa Fe Stockyards in Flagstaff.

The castle has secret passageways and seven bathrooms. The dungeon is the bar. Copenhaver moved in about 1978 after twelve years of construction. As is the case for so many Camelback developers before him, Dr. Copenhaver was not able to enjoy the fruits of his labor. By 1987 his company DentaHealth was in bankruptcy. Copenhaver put his castle on the market in 1985 for $7 million. In 1989 Copenhaver Castle was sold to Jerry Mitchell for $985,000.

Copenhaver joins a long list of colorful Camelback "characters." He married three times and is the father of three adult children. Copenhaver lived in the castle with 31-year-old Beverly Rodrigues, an attractive lady of Portuguese ancestry who, according to newspaper reports at the time, didn't see the castle until it was finished. While living in the castle Copenhaver had elaborate parties and offered tours to the public.

CUDIA CITY

At one time, the desert lands around Camelback served as a backdrop for Western movies. In 1938, Salvatore Pace Bond-anza Cudia built a movie studio and dinner theater on 160 acres just north of Camelback Road at 40th Street. The 1950s television series "26 Men," based on the Arizona Rangers, was produced at Cudia City.

I recall Cudia City was a popular recreation spot for young Phoenicians in the 1950s. It burned to the ground in 1959 but was soon rebuilt.

THE ANIMALS OF CAMELBACK

As we descend to the main trail, we notice Harris hawks and peregrine falcons circling above us. The peregrine falcons live in the rocky cliffs of Echo Canyon. These rare birds are among the fastest on earth when diving. I've also seen great horned owls

ABOVE: *Water in a desert tinaja. Photo by J.R. Norton.*
INSET: *S.P.D. Cudia, circa 1950.*

nesting in the nearby cliffs. We see a hummingbird. They are abundant on Camelback, particularly near the shaded cliffs. Camelback is one of the best places for birding in the Phoenix area.

Not only are birds abundant on Camelback, but other desert wildlife is, as well. The desert animals fall into the three categories of endurers, evaders and escapers. The largest class, naturally, would be the animals that endure. Their primary defense mechanism is avoiding the heat of the sun. Most of the animals spend the day in burrows or out of the direct sunlight and carry on most of their activity at night when temperatures are low and humidity is high.

The evaders consist primarily of snakes who have managed to hibernate during much of the cold winter and they stay out of

ABOVE: *Getting exercise. Photo by Bryan Casebolt.*
OPPOSITE: *Sunset on the walls of the head. Photo by J.R. Norton.*

the direct sunlight for most of the summer.

The escape animals are those that can go into a dormant phase for literally months or years only to come alive when the rains come and moisture is available. Some desert animals such as certain rodents can literally produce most of their water needs from the food that they eat. However, the desert animals learn the location of the springs or tinajas, which are rock holes in the washes that hold water in pools for long periods of time.

On Camelback there are several areas where the water stands for some time after a rain in rock hollows that are shaded most of the day. Camelback is home to an amazing array of animals that survive even with the significant development surrounding the mountain.

Camelback is alive with animals. Most of them are in their burrows during the day while humans take over the surface of the trails for their hiking and mountain climbing activities. The most common animal seen during the day is the Harris antelope

ground squirrel, which looks like a chipmunk but is in fact a ground squirrel. They are active during the entire year and can be seen darting back and forth, and in and out of the rocks looking for food and enjoying the activity that goes on the mountain every day. They have natural predators—the hawks, the coyotes, the snakes and other animals—but they are common throughout the mountain. There are also a desert cottontail rabbits, jackrabbits, grey fox, raccoons, pack rats and a wonderful array of birds that live on and near the mountain.

Near the summit of the mountains there is a huge population of birds that live in the 200 foot sheer northeastern face, just below the summit of the hump. Over 30 species of birds regularly spend time on Camelback, including a large hummingbird population which is attracted to the abundant flowers on the shaded north side of the head of Camelback.

In addition to these well known animals, there are several kinds of toads that live on Camelback, including: Couch's spadefoot toad, Sonoran Desert toads, Great Plains toads, Woodhouse's toads and red-spotted toads. While Camelback might seem an unlikely place for these amphibians, they are able to burrow deep into the sands of the washes around Camelback and remain dormant until the rains come.

There are numerous kinds of lizards on Camelback. The chuckwalla is the largest and best known. It is often mistaken for a gila monster due to the splotchy, orange skin of the chuckwalla, but they are quite harmless vegetarians.

There are also side-blotched lizards, desert spiny lizards, banded geckos, zebra tail lizards, western whiptail lizards and collared lizards.

Camelback is home to two kinds of rattlesnakes—the tiger rattler and the speckled rattler. There are also gopher snakes (sometimes called bull snakes), common king snakes (often confused with the poisonous, but rare, coral snake), ground snake, blind snake, long-nosed snake, coachwhip snake, and the Sonoran whipsnake.

The beautiful, but venomous gila monster is also found on Camelback. Since these reclusive animals spend about 95 percent of their time in their burrows, they are seldom seen.

All of these animals basically spend much of their life out of sight in the burrows and rock piles of Camelback and find a way to enjoy the shade that Camelback provides due to the abundance of rocks and steep rock walls that afford better shade than

ABOVE: *Dudleya, a desert succulent, on Camelback.*
Photo by J.R. Norton. OPPOSITE: *Dudleya—a shady spot*
makes it possible. Photo by J.R. Norton.

most areas of the Salt River Valley.

In hiking the mountain you can always see birds circling. Large hawks provide an inspiring view as they catch the thermals around the mountain and circle looking for food.

Camelback has become the favorite birding spot for local enthusiasts, but the best spot is the Echo Canyon area where the volume of hikers is substantially less then either of the main trails. But at any point on Camelback there are many birds to observe throughout.

At the insect level, carpenter bees which look like a black bumble bee are frequently seen flying on a solitary basis around the mountain. These solitary carpenter bees are quite harmless and do not attack humans.

In addition, there is a substantial population of bats living in the caves and rocks of Camelback. A careful look in some of the caves of the Camel's Head reveals the droppings of the bats. The bats enjoy the shade and safety of the caves high on the mountain.

There are several hives of honey bees on the mountain and they afford occasional challenges for rock climbers who will encounter a beehive high up on a rock wall. The shaded caves and walls of Camelback have long been a favorite spot for local honey bees who also find a generous harvest from both the desert flowers of Camelback and the surrounding residential areas.

Larger animals such as coyotes and even bobcats have been seen on Camelback. My sister, Anne, who lives on the slopes of Camelback has had to secure her pet food because the raccoons and foxes from Camelback came on a regular basis to consume any that was left outside. Another friend found a bobcat at his house one morning but the animals are increasingly adapting to living with the humans that surround the mountains. The coyotes appear quite relaxed as they wander through the residential areas on their way up and down to their mountain hideaways on Camelback and their other surrounding mountains.

Bats leave for an evening of feasting on the insects that abound on the golf courses around the foot of Camelback. I have often seen bats flying around my home that probably came from nearby Camelback. On one occasion we came home to find that the baby sitter had captured a bat in the house. No doubt a visitor from nearby Camelback mountain.

We often see rock squirrels during the day. But most desert animals are full of activity during the evening. As soon as the sun comes back they take refuge in their burrows to wait for another evening of intense activity.

MOSSES, LICHENS AND LIVERWORTS

As we walk along the trail towards Echo Canyon with the sheer walls towering above us, we are in one of the most continuously shaded areas of Camelback. This is an ideal environment for the growth of some of the most primitive plants found on Camelback— mosses, lichens and liverworts.

LICHENS—NATURE'S ABSTRACT ART

The lichens of Camelback form a kind of covering on the north sides of the rocks in varying hues of green, yellow and orange. Many of the lichen displays are so beautiful that they appear to have been put on the rocks as abstract paintings. In fact, they are living things—a combination of algae and fungus. They play an important role in breaking up the rocks and creating the soil that sustains the plants that grow on the mountain. Depending on whether the lichens are wet or dry, some can change in color

from yellow to green. They create colorful displays on the rocks as you climb on the trails of Camelback.

MOSSES AND LICHENS—FELLOW TRAVELERS

One of the most enjoyable things for me has been to watch for the tiny mosses that often grow with the lichens. There are many kinds of mosses on Camelback. During most of the dry periods they simply appear to be a black or brown plant, or not even plants at all. When the rains come these mosses are converted to a brilliant display of various colors of green and literally change the color and feeling of the entire mountain. One of the most satisfying experiences is to climb Camelback after a rain and see the mountain take on a lush appearance. The mosses of Camelback are reminiscent of a rain forest.

LIVERWORTS—EASY TO OVERLOOK

When Camelback is dry, the soil in shaded areas often has little areas of clusters of black lines that appear to be mineral deposits. These black clusters do not at all seem notable and literally fade into the background. After a rain, these clusters of black lines turn into tiny bright-green, linear leaves that appear to be glued to the ground. These tiny plants are called liverworts. They are a bryophyte or a kind of moss. In their green, active phase they bear not even the slightest resemblance to the cluster of black lines from whence they came.

THE QUINTESSENTIAL NECKING SPOT

In the 1940s and '50s, the teenagers used to "ride the bumps" on McDonald Drive—driving fast enough over the rolling hills to get airborne for a few seconds before reaching the next hump. Riding the bumps was the typical prelude to stopping in Echo Canyon for the real purpose of the trip, which was to neck. Phoenix teen-agers during the 1940s and 50s all knew that one of the best necking spots in town was Echo Canyon. The beautiful, natural setting provided the perfect spot for high-school kids to neck. While this sort of activity may seem "tame" in the salacious 1990s, necking in Echo Canyon was a high point during my own high-school era.

DUNCAN MacDONALD—SHORT-CHANGED

McDonald Drive borders the northern base of Camelback, carrying with it a rich history of the early part of this century. One of the men who placed a lasting mark on the development around Camelback was Duncan MacDonald whose name marks the major road running along the north side of Camelback. Unfortunately MacDonald is misspelled as if to add a little injury to the memory of a man who did so much for development near Camelback only to have others harvest the benefit of his work. This is the treatment so many Camelback developers have received.

Duncan was born in New Zealand in 1876 to a Scottish family. He married an English girl and had three children. Duncan learned to be a master of ornamental plaster. He worked doing elaborate plaster sculptures on public buildings and churches in Australia. When work slowed in Australia he moved to South Africa where his wife died, leaving him with the three children who he placed in a convent. Duncan worked wherever he could, including Egypt.

The 1906 San Francisco earthquake created a big demand for construction work and Duncan MacDonald moved to California, leaving the children with relatives in Australia.

In 1910 he married a California girl and moved to Arizona. Once in Arizona he sent for his three children and added two more by his new wife. In Phoenix he established a plastering business and did some of the most beautiful plaster work in Arizona. He did the fabulous plaster work inside the Orpheum Theater which opened in 1929 with Clark Gable and Mae West appearing in person for the opening which featured their movie, *I'm No Angel*.

In 1919 he acquired a 120-acre tract next to the land owned by Jessie Benton Evans on Camelback Road. In 1928 and 1930 MacDonald filed two subdivision plats on his land north of Camelback. In Glencoe Highlands subdivided in 1928 he named the street on the western border MacDonald Drive (now Hilltop) and the other streets for his three girls, Jean, Helen, and Elsie.

In the '20s Duncan purchased a substantial amount of land just north and east of Camelback. In the late '20s he rented horses and a scraper and developed a north-south road on the eastern base of Camelback Mountain to his property. He named the road Invergordon after a town in Scotland. He also scraped an east-west road on the border of his property, which became McDonald Drive. He built a house on his property north of Camelback, which

A few of the flowers of Camelback. Photos by Bryan Casebolt (upper left and right); Bob Rink (lower left); J.R. Norton (lower right).

Mexican gold poppy.

Climbing milkweed.

Blue-dicks, or Covena.

Globe mallow.

ABOVE: *Running on Camelback. Photo by Bryan Casebolt.*
OPPOSITE: *Liverworts in their active phase after a rain. Photo by J.R. Norton.*

was the first fine home of the area.

MacDonald lost his Camelback property during the Depression of the 1930s for inability to pay 25 cents per acre taxes. Hard times also hit his plastering business. But MacDonald went on his entrepreneurial way in spite of these setbacks. He became the first to put perlite on the market commercially. Perlite block became one of the important building materials in Arizona. He died in Phoenix in 1949.

MacDonald's wife, Fay, lived another 16 years. She played a significant role in area development. She was secretary to the project engineer of Roosevelt Dam and secretary of both the Roosevelt Conservation District and the Camelback Water Conservation District.

FROM ECHO CANYON TO THE NOSE

From the Echo Canyon Bowl, the trail climbs up slightly to a spectacular pass overlooking the highrise district of central Phoenix. A sharp rock wall on the left and a rounded sandstone formation to the

right provide the perfect contrast of a wild desert mountain in a modern metropolis.

GODDARD SAVES THE CAMEL'S NOSE

Below us, there is a field of boulders resting on a grassy slope that leads to the houses surrounding the mountain. Directly below us is the home of Sam Goddard, former Arizona Governor, and his wife, Julia. They have lived near the nose of Camelback for many years. In December 1983 they made a gift of 3.3 acres on the western slope of Camelback to the city of Phoenix for an addition to the Camelback Mountain Preserve. This land connects to the trail to Bobby's Rock, a popular technical climbing spot, and to Echo Canyon. The Goddard gift includes some of the most beautiful cliffs and boulders on the mountain. In a heavy rain the brief waterfalls that cascade into the Goddard property are some of the most impressive in Arizona.

THE FLOWERS OF CAMELBACK

While the grasses and flowers on Camelback come mostly in the spring, there are tiny flowers and interesting displays of plant life going on during every season. Camelback is a garden, a desert garden with one of the greatest varieties of Sonoran Desert plants for a small area. The sad thing is that many of those that climb Camelback are unaware of the dazzling array of plant life that they are observing.

THE ANNUAL WILDFLOWER SEASON

The winter rains provide a more-thorough soaking of the ground, which can lead to an incredible display of spring wildflowers on Camelback. The saguaro, paloverde and brittlebush also bloom every year. The variety ranges from the eye-catching display of white blossoms atop the saguaro to tiny flowers which may only be 1/16 of an inch in diameter. There are two distinct flowering seasons following the winter and the summer storms.

The flowers of Camelback bloom in a sequence that provides new varieties of flowers during a good part of the year. The desert lupine is among the first to flower just after the new year and often lasts until May. The brittlebush usually follows in March with a brilliant display. The Mexican gold poppy starts in February and lasts about three months. The paloverde start blooming in March—first on the lower slopes and then progressing up the mountain. All in all, Camelback offers a fine, natural flower garden.

UNUSUAL CLASSIFICATIONS FOR PLANTS

The Sonoran Desert and Camelback have three general classifications of plants: endurers, evaders and escapers. The largest group of plants can be classified as endurers. Examples would be cacti, the little leaf paloverde tree and the creosote bush. These plants have developed adaptations that allow them to survive under the harshest conditions. For example, many of them have developed either the ability to build the plant material in the skin of the plant, such as the cacti and little leaf paloverde. Others have developed special coverings on their skin that allow them to hold moisture, lower the rate of transpiration and absorb moisture either directly through the skin of the plant or shallow roots that can absorb even the tiniest amount of moisture. These adaptations create some of the most beautiful plants of the Sonoran Desert.

THE INCREDIBLE SELF-PRUNING PALOVERDE

The most common tree of the Sonoran Desert is the foothill or little leaf paloverde. Camelback Mountain is covered with literally thousands of little leaf paloverde trees. This is probably the most common plant on the mountain and is by far the most common tree in the Sonoran Desert. The paloverde trees on Camelback can grow to a height of over 20 feet in some cases. It is also one of the most interesting plants of this Sonoran Desert is the paloverde. In Spanish it means green stick. This is a very appropriate name as about 90 percent of all the photosynthesis takes place in the branches and stems rather than the tiny leaves which only come out after a rain.

The paloverde is what is called a self-pruning tree. During periods of drought the branches die and

eventually fall off. So, you can look at the ends of the branches of the paloverde trees on Camelback and determine how wet the recent period has been. In late April and May the little leaf paloverde flowers into a pale yellow display which covers Camelback Mountain in a beautiful yellow bath. The paloverde tree creates abundant seeds which are an important source of food for the rodents, beetles, and other desert animals. These seeds can survive for long periods of time and come alive after any soaking rain. Paloverde are important desert nurse plants which provide shade and refuge that allow other plants such as saguaros to get a start in the desert without the heat of the sun.

The paloverde is most abundant along the washes of the Sonoran Desert and on Camelback the paloverde delineate the path of water as it descends the mountain from the rains. As you look at Camelback you can follow the drainage patterns by the concentration of the little leaf paloverde trees. Each blossom of the paloverde tree has four pale yellow petals and one white petal. All of the trees in an area will flower at the same time. Even in the driest years the paloverde will put on a brilliant display of yellow on Camelback.

THE CREOSOTE BUSH OR "LITTLE STINKER"

The creosote bush is one of the most abundant plants on Camelback. In fact, it is the most successful plant of the American desert. The creosote bush, with its dark gray stems and small bright green leaves, covers Camelback Mountain. The distinctive smell of the desert after a rain comes from the resin or varnish that covers its leaves and helps the plant retain moisture.

While the smell of the creosote bush is very satisfying to humans, it is not attractive to animals. The Mexicans gave it the name "Little Stinker." The creosote bush has an extensive root system which is able to soak up even the tiniest amount of rain and provides the creosote with the ability to survive even extreme drought. In some places in the American desert the creosote bush is about the only plant that survives in great numbers. Its extensive root system provides the structural support for underground burrows that allow desert animals to beat the heat by going underground where the temperature only varies slightly from summer to winter and provides

ABOVE: *The tiny Cryptantha.* OPPOSITE: *Giant boulders along the Camel's Head Trail. Photos by J.R. Norton.*

a pleasant temperature even during the hottest periods of the summer. The creosote bush yields abundant yellow flowers which attract numerous insects including many kinds of bees. The fruits are a small, fuzzy white ball which is a good source of food for many desert dwelling animals. The smell of the creosote bush after a summer rain is one of the most satisfying experiences of the Sonoran Desert.

EVADE AND LIVE

The evaders are those plants that find other ways to get moisture. They hibernate during periods of intense heat, losing most of their leaves. Others roll or fold their leaves so there is less surface water loss. One of the best examples of this type of plant is the ocotillo, a spindly plant that grows on Camelback and elsewhere in the Sonoran Desert. It will lose all of its leaves during the summer or other harsh periods but quickly develops an entirely new suit of green leaves almost every time it rains.

TINY FLOWERS AND LOTS OF BURRS

An evader plant is the triangle-leaf bursage. The bursage is one of the real worker plants of the Sonoran Desert. This small shrub with gray-green leaves not unlike the color of the brittlebush leaves provides one of the great ecological tasks of the Sonoran Desert. It is a nurse plant for numerous cacti and other seedlings which gain shade and get their start in life from the hard working bursage shrub. The bursage is little appreciated. It has beautiful yellow flowers, but they are very small and are hardly visible. These tiny flowers get their pollination from the breezes blowing across the desert. You must carefully look for the rows of vertical flowers that later develop into the burrs. These burrs are somewhat irritating to humans passing through the desert, but they provide a rich source of food for ants, rodents and small birds. The hard working bursage plant again evades the heat of the Sonoran Desert by losing almost all of its leaves during a dry period only to develop a handsome, new set of foliage when the wetter season allows. Camelback is covered with many bursage plants, and it is fun to look underneath the plants and see how often the bursage is nursing another weaker desert plant.

THE BRIGHTEST YELLOW OF SPRING

One of the most common low plants on Camelback is the brittlebush which is another evad-

Filaree. Photo by J.R. Norton.

Bursage. Photo by Bob Rink.

er. It is a dome-shaped bush about three feet high with gray-green leaves. The brittlebush sheds many of its leaves during the dry period and looks largely like a clump of sticks.

When the rains come it produces a rich foliage which in the spring flowers into the brightest display of yellow that is seen on the Sonoran Desert. Camelback has thousands of brittlebush, providing a

Wallflower. Photo by J.R. Norton.

Desert bluebells or phacelia. Photo by Bryan Casebolt.

Desert buckwheat. Photo by J.R. Norton.

Fiddleneck. Photo by J.R. Norton.

Silver Puff. Photo by Bryan Casebolt.

Star Point. Photo by Bob Rink.

bright yellow cover during March and April. The flowers grow at the end of long stems, which are a few inches beyond the main foliage of the plant to make them readily accessible to pollinating insects.

If you examine the gray-green leaves closely you will see that they are covered with microscopic white hairs which are a form of desert adaptation that filter and reflect the direct sunlight and reduce the water loss from the leaves. Brittlebush is an excellent example of an evader plant in the Sonoran Desert, as it loses its leaves and slows its growth to a standstill during the dry periods. The stems of the brittlebush produce a gum which was highly valued as incense by early Catholic priests. The gum was also used by the Indians for chewing and as a salve to relieve pain.

Boulder Canyon. Photo by J.R. Norton.

THE SHORT COURSE IN PLANT I.D.

The four plants that we have discussed, the little leaf paloverde, the brittlebush, the bursage and the creosote comprise the vast majority of all the number of plants of Arizona's Sonoran Desert, perhaps as high as 90 percent of the number of plants. Over the years I have enjoyed telling people that I can teach them quickly how to identify 90 percent of the plants of the Sonoran Desert. This seems like a big task, until they realize that once you learn these four plants, you can identify the vast preponderance of all of the plants that you will see in the Sonoran Desert. Of course, there are hundreds of varieties of plants, but these occur in much smaller numbers.

PLANT ESCAPES ON CAMELBACK

The final classification is the escaper. These are annual plants which each year grow and flourish during the wet seasons, create seeds and quickly die as the hot sun takes the temperatures above a level they can tolerate. These plants create abundant seeds which sometimes lie dormant for many years only to come alive again when the conditions are right. The wildflowers, which create the fantastic displays of color during the springtime, are largely composed of escapers.

TEDDY BEAR CHOLLA

The most feared cactus of Camelback is the teddy bear cholla. The sharp, pale, golden spines have microscopic barbs going in the other direction, making it almost impossible to remove cholla spines from your body. While the teddy bear cholla is not technically the "Jumping Cactus" it behaves like one. The balls that comprise the stems quickly come off into the skin or clothing if the hiker even brushes the teddy bear cholla. The teddy bear cholla does produce a beautiful, pale green flower in the spring but they should be watched from a respectful distance. The chollas do very well in intense sunlight and can be seen on the south-facing slopes of Camelback. The sharp spines of the cholla provide an excellent natural air conditioning by shading the plant from the sun and wind.

THE BUCKHORN CHOLLA

The buckhorn cholla can be seen along the trail to the top of Camelback. This cholla has stick-like limbs, which have the appearance of being the antlers of a deer. The flowers are a bright yellow-orange and bloom in April and May. This cholla is not nearly as fearsome as the teddy bear cholla.

The stems can be eaten as a vegetable, but only after the spines are burned off. On Camelback, they are usually about three feet tall.

THE HEDGEHOG CACTUS

The hedgehog cactus can be seen best along the Cholla Trail, where it grows six to ten inches high, with long spines and a striking magenta flower with a green stigma. The flowers, which bloom in April and May, are large and are among the most beautiful desert flowers. The sharp spines together with the bright flowers make the hedgehog one of the most vivid plants on Camelback.

THE FISHHOOK OR PINCUSHION CACTUS

The pincushion cacti grow to a height of six inches in clusters of three or four and are often hidden by a nurse plant. This delicate cactus has curved spines, which look like fish hooks. The scientific name for this cactus is *mammillaria* due to the nipple-like projections on the stems.

BARREL CACTUS

Barrel cacti are common on the trails of Camelback. They grow from a few inches to several feet in height and look indeed like a stretched-out barrel. The flowers are a yellow-orange and bloom from spring into the summer months. They are sometimes called compass barrels because they lean slightly towards the south. The spines have a fish-hook look. The younger plants have hues of brilliant red, making the barrel one of the more unusual plants along the Camelback trails. Often, the barrel can be seen growing out of a rock that would appear not to have any nutrient soil to support the barrel, but these are hardy cacti and seem to be able to grow even in the rockiest spots on Camelback.

THE ARIZONA CANAL—PIONEER INGENUITY

One of the largest desert cities in the world teems below us. Yet, the Valley floor is a green carpet of trees, hedges and well-manicured lawns. Farther out on the horizon, fields of cotton and alfalfa stretch as far as we can see. One of the things that made life in this arid environment possible was the importation of water via canals that had been used 500 years ear-lier by the Hohokam people. Snaking around the base of Camelback Mountain is the Arizona Canal, built just over a century ago.

Development of the Phoenix metropolitan area really began in earnest more than one hundred years ago with the development by private companies of canals to bring water from the Salt River for irrigation. William John Murphy had a profound influence on the modern development of lands near Camelback. He was born in New Hartford, New York, in 1839 to parents who had just immigrat-ed from Ireland.

During the Civil War, W.J. Murphy joined the Union Army and quickly rose to Junior Second Lieutenant and fought with

ABOVE: *An early view of the canal and the mountain, circa 1900.*
Arizona Historical Society. INSET: *W.J. Murphy. Arizona Department of Library, Archives and Public Records.*

Praying Monk. Photo by Bryan Casebolt.

Sherman's army. By the end of the war he was an Acting Assistant Adjutant General. After the war he married and taught school in Nashville, Tennessee. After six years of marriage and two children, his wife died. He married a second time in 1874 and that union bore four children. Murphy became a partner in a hardware and lumber store in Pontiac, Illinois.

About 1879, he got into the business of railroad grading. He did railroad work in both Illinois and Nebraska, before moving to Colorado, New Mexico and Arizona. By 1881 he was at work in Flagstaff, Arizona. In the 1880s Flagstaff was a wild frontier town. During one week while Murphy was in Flagstaff there were seven men shot in saloon fights. In 1881 and 1882 he worked on grading for the main line of the Atlantic and Pacific Railroad.

At age 44, W. J. Murphy moved to the Salt River Valley to build the Arizona Canal. Murphy's saga would be one of the most unusual and interesting in Arizona's colorful history.

The Arizona Canal Company had already been formed, water rights obtained and plans for the canal developed. The plans were bold. A 40-mile-long canal would run from the confluence of the Salt and Verde rivers to New River. Irrigation water would be available for 100,000 acres.

The route of the Arizona Canal would wrap around the southern slopes of Camelback and would open that entire area to development. Murphy agreed to build the entire canal in exchange for stock and bonds and water rights of the Arizona Canal Company.

It was up to Murphy to sell bonds to get money to operate. Soon after signing the contract Murphy had second thoughts. He wrote to his wife: "If I could do so without loss of credit and honor I would let the money expended go and throw up the enterprise and spend the summer with you. But it would be disastrous to my business reputation and in honor I could not do it."

He immediately contacted his former subcontractors and got them involved in the job. By 1883, according to Murphy's grandson, an estimated 225 mule teams and 450 men were at work building the canal.

Murphy had constant problems raising money to continue the work. Local banks were not large enough to provide adequate financing. He frequently traveled to California to obtain money. His contract required he reach a certain point by a set date or lose the contract. A newspaper article described efforts to sabotage Murphy by staging a strike during a rain-

A postcard from Phoenix proudly displaying the canal and Camelback Mountain.

storm when telegraph lines were down. Murphy met the deadline with just two hours to spare.

Upon completion of the canal, the *Gazette* ran an article on June 1, 1885 that compared the canal to the Erie Canal of New York: "Water flows gracefully and evenly through its entire length of forty-one miles. . . . It's a grand improvement and although of a public nature it has been constructed entirely by private means. . .due to the energy, enterprise and great business capacity of a few men. "

DROUGHT HITS THE ARIZONA CANAL

The Arizona Canal made the lands around Camelback readily accessible to residents. As so often has been the case with Camelback development, things didn't simply go merrily along. When the Arizona Canal and other canals were built, the U.S. Department of Interior said the Salt and Verde rivers could irrigate 250,000 acres without storage. Mother Nature didn't see it that way. By the turn of the century there was a period of sharply reduced water flows. Litigation ensued. As president and chief shareholder in the Arizona Canal Company,

Murphy had a vital interest in these water rights. Nevertheless, litigation was settled with a decree that reduced the water available to the Arizona Canal Company.

Murphy saw the need for permanent water storage. An expedition was sent up the Salt River to find a dam site. John Norton, grandfather of the John Norton who has taken so many of the pictures for this book, was part of that expedition. Murphy paid for much of the expenses, including those of Norton.

PRIVATE MONEY FOR A DAM

Murphy tried to privately raise the money for the dam. He spent a year in Europe trying to get funds, to no avail. While these efforts were going on, the affairs of the Arizona Canal company declined. In 1897, Murphy lost control of the Arizona Canal Company and the Arizona Improvement Company.

But Murphy continued to work for irrigation and water storage. He had boundless energy and enthusiasm for new tasks. One of these efforts included developing a forest reserve north of the Valley to protect the watershed. Murphy met with President

PREVIOUS PAGE LEFT: *On the ridge of the Camel's Head.*
PREVIOUS PAGE RIGHT: *Downtown from Camel's foot. Photos by Bryan Casebolt.* ABOVE: *The Camel's foot from the top of Echo Canyon. Photo by Bryan Casebolt.* OPPOSITE: *The Echo Canyon Bowl Association, circa 1926. Arizona Collection, Arizona State University Libraries.*

Theodore Roosevelt, the U.S. Interior Secretary and a Senator Payson from Arizona.

According to a newspaper account, Roosevelt said, "Murphy, who do you represent?" Mr. Murphy replied, "I represent 60,000 people in the Salt River Valley whose welfare depends on the protection of the watershed of the Salt and Verde Rivers." Then Roosevelt said, "State your case." Murphy stated that all the owners of the timberland within the proposed forest reserves had signed agreements to take government land script in exchange for their lands in the reserves and that there was nothing now in the way of a presidential order to create a forest reserve.

After consulting others in the room, and hearing an objection from the Santa Fe Railway, Roosevelt rose and said to the Secretary of the Interior, "Mr. Secretary, you will please see that this order is made immediately. Good day, Gentlemen. I am glad to have met you."

The effort now was to obtain federal funding for a dam and reclamation project.

Murphy's goal was to have the government buy the existing canal companies rather then build a new delivery system.

When negotiations became deadlocked, Murphy supplied the last $40,000 to bring the parties together. A Phoenix newspaper reported the 1906 deal in large type: "CANALS ARE SOLD."

Thus, Murphy did more than anyone else to bring water to Camelback, which made possible the development of the citrus groves of the Arcadia neighborhood at the southern base of the mountain, as well as other developments around Camelback.

The water supply in the Arizona Canal became even more reliable with the completion of Roosevelt Dam in 1910.

With the completion of the road along the Arizona Canal in 1885, Camelback Mountain was readily accessible to the citizens of newly founded Phoenix. Trips to Camelback for picnics and other desert recreation soon became popular.

Even with the development of the Arizona Canal and other canals, the population of Phoenix was only 5,500 in 1900, and Camelback was eight miles from the center of town—very much in the distant suburbs. Once the Theodore Roosevelt Dam project was announced, farmers flocked to Phoenix. By 1910 the population of Phoenix had doubled to 11,000 people.

CONCERTS IN ECHO CANYON

The Echo Canyon Bowl Association was formed in 1926 with the objective of becoming the Hollywood Bowl of Phoenix. In addition to Rudolph Balke, who served as president, association members were: Ralph Murphy, vice president and general manager; and Russ Tatum as attorney and a director. The purpose of the association as set forth in their 1927 annual report was "to promote the public welfare of Phoenix, Maricopa County, and the state of Arizona, by developing the historic Echo Canyon into an outdoor amphitheater to accommodate large public gatherings that could not otherwise be accommodated." The land was provided by W.O. O'Brien, who had filed a homestead on the property in 1906. Both Murphy and Tatum were actively promoting the area and the Bowl seemed like a fine addition. It would help sell Tatum's land to the north, and Murphy would take his guests from the Ingleside

Near Echo Canyon. Photo by Bryan Casebolt.

resort there for picnics, recitals and dance exhibitions by the Indian employees of the resort.

Phoenix was enthusiastic about the Bowl. I.E. Behymer, father of the Hollywood Bowl, came to Phoenix and said, "Nature creates better sounding boards and better acoustic conditions than man has ever imitated and at Echo Canyon nature has, to use the vernacular, done herself proud."

In December 1926, Mary Kathryn Young, president of the Phoenix Music Club, had tested the acoustics while architects and other Bowl enthusiasts listened at various distances. They concluded that 10,000 people could be accommodated at the Bowl with good quality sound.

An architect was hired to design the Bowl, including seating. A wooden stage was built by the association and a foot bridge over the arroyo. Phoenix Mayor Frank A. Jefferson said the Bowl would provide "unusually fine entertainment at lost cost." He was right. For most events, admission was 50 cents. Arizona Tours would bus patrons to the Bowl for $1, including admission.

A statewide fund-raising effort started in 1927,

but the Depression hit Arizona before the job was complete. The last report of the Bowl Association was filed in 1930.

During the Bowl's brief tenure there were good crowds and successful concerts. The 158th Infantry Band was rained out, but came back a week later and played in spite of another rain. On the third week the band played to an audience of 2,000 people. On January 1, 1927, a 40-piece orchestra, a 70-person Mormon Choir and seven Hopi dancers performed. A number of other concerts took place in 1927. I have talked to people who participated in school programs produced in Echo Canyon. Use of the Bowl for cultural events continued sporadically into the 1930s. Reportedly, it was offered to the City of Phoenix for a minimal cost but the city declined. Eventually, like so much other property in Phoenix, it was lost for failure to pay taxes of $235, according to Ralph Murphy's daughter.

In 1943, Brooklyn Trust attempted to determine if there was any value in the Echo Canyon Bowl Association and received a letter from the Arizona Corporation Commission saying: "This association never functioned as it was intended to do. During the period of 'boon-doggling' the Bowl itself was supplied with concrete seats by one of the Federal Relief Agencies but to the best of my knowledge, the only functions they have ever held there are early morning devotionals on Easter Sunday. I note from the record that the affairs of this association were in the hands of Mr. Russ F. Tatum. . ."

The Echo Canyon Bowl Association is another of Camelback's might-have-beens. It is a great venue for concerts, but as with so many Camelback dreams, other forces intervened. I've discussed with several residents of Echo Canyon the idea of reviving the Bowl Association for an annual charity fund-raising event. As I continue up the trail, into an area that is almost always shaded, and wonder: Could the Bowl Association find new life? Just maybe.

ALMOST AN INDIAN RESERVATION

The fledgling town of Phoenix was just getting its start in 1879, when on Jan. 10 that year, President Rutherford B. Hayes expanded the reservations of the Salt River Pima and Maricopa Indians. The one-paragraph order simply stated, "It is hereby ordered that all public lands embraced within the following boundaries lying within the territory of Arizona . . . are hereby withdrawn from sale and are set apart for

MAYNARD DIXON

Maynard Dixon was born in Fresno, California, in 1875. He had only three months of formal art training in 1893 at San Francisco's Mark Hopkins Institute of Art. Maynard Dixon was a regionalist concentrating on the landscapes of Southern California, Nevada, Utah, Arizona and New Mexico.

In the 1890s he was one of the country's leading purveyors of Old West nostalgic images. For much of his life, Dixon roamed the West by every means of transportation, painting every Western subject he could find.

Dixon painted numerous Arizona scenes, including Camelback. He died on November 13, 1946, just after completing a major mural of the Grand Canyon.

He wrote the following verse in 1921:

O, I am Maynard Dixon,
And I live out here, alone
With pencil and pen and paint-brush
And a camp stool for my throne
King of the desert country
Holding a magic key
To the world's magnificent treasure
None can unlock but me!
At times come terrible moments
When desire fills full my soul,
And women and wine and cities
Seem a compelling goal;—
But I wake with a start to be desert
And its lovely vistas unfurled,——
I'd rather be Maynard Dixon,
Than anyone else in the world!

—*Desert Dreams: The Art and Life of Maynard Dixon*

ABOVE: *A concert in Echo Canyon, circa 1927. Arizona Collection, Arizona State University Libraries.* INSET: *Charles Poston, circa 1890.* OPPOSITE: *Ocotillo in Echo Canyon. Photo by J.R. Norton.*

the use of the Pima and Maricopa Indians in addition to their present reservation in said territory."

In January 1879 the same Charles Poston who started the Arizona mining boom was now serving as the register of the U.S. land office at Florence. The stage was set for Poston to play his most important role in a legendary life of influence in Arizona. It was Poston's job to record filings on ownership rights of the Homestead Act of 1862 and Desert Land Act of 1877, which increased the allowable homestead in the Phoenix area from 160 acres to 640 acres.

The president's order had been reported in the *Salt River Herald* on January 14, 1879. Poston received his official notification on January 27, 1879, and immediately marked his maps according to his instructions, which were to "make proper

annotations upon the township plat" of lands falling within the enlarged reservation, and "to protect the reservation by refusing to allow any further entries or things upon the lands."

To Poston the enlarged reservation was shocking—it encompassed about one million acres, completely engulfing Camelback Mountain. The new reservation started at the mouth of the Salt River and included most of the current urbanized area, including all of Phoenix below what is now Northern Avenue and most of Tempe, Mesa, Chandler, Scottsdale, Camelback Mountain and two miles on either side of the Salt River to the White Mountain Apache Reservation. At present, more than 2.5 million people live on the lands of this expanded reservation. Then, 5,000 "hard-working citizens" and only a few hundred Indians occupied the same lands.

POSTON—THE PROTECTOR OF PHOENIX

Poston sprang into action. He realized that if this order remained in effect, settlement of the Salt River Valley was at an end for all practical purposes. By the

Hiking in Echo Canyon. Photo by Bryan Casebolt.

next day he had written a letter to Arizona Governor John C. Freemont. "To his Excellency, General J.C. Freemont, Governor of Arizona: . . . Being loth to impose additional labor upon your already over-taxed time at the present moment, but the gravity of the calamity to this people of the Salt River Valley, and the imminent danger it involves of a conflict between the settlers and the Indians will induce you to sympathize with my apprehensions," Poston wrote. Then, in intricate detail, he outlined the exact lands that had been given back to the first peoples to inhabit the region.

"In all cases the settlers have contributed something to the treasury and in the desert land entries 25 cents per acre have been paid on a contract which the government now repudiates," Poston implored. "The reservation embraces the heart of the agricultural land of the Territory settled by an industrious and thrifty community of good citizens, augmenting rapidly the wealth and population of the territory. The thrifty town of Phoenix is now in the center of an Indian reservation and the whole population of the Salt River Valley are disenfranchised by an executive order, and brought under the federal governing Indian reservations."

Near the nose of the Camel. Photo by Bryan Casebolt.

Poston also decried the newly imposed federal fine of $5,000 with imprisonment for selling "spirituous liquors" on the new reservation. "Merchants cannot continue trade without a license from an Indian agent," Poston complained. "I am at a loss to conceive what malignant influence could have been exercised upon the President to induce the issuance of an executive order leaving such manifest injustice. . . . The territory is smothered with 'Reservations.' "

Poston's letter was published on February 1, 1879, in the *Salt River Herald*. It was no accident because Poston had sent a copy of his letter to Governor Freemont to all of the newspapers in the Arizona territory. One of the influential papers in the territory was the *Miner*, published in Prescott. Editor Charles Beach hated Indians and reflected his feelings in an editorial on January 30, 1879, which stated in part, "The Pima Indians should be taken from their present location on Salt River, and placed by themselves, where they will not come in contact with white people. The lands they are settled upon are owned by bona fide citizens, who located them, and are kept from their peaceful occupation by old Chin-chi-a-

cum, one of the meanest old wrenches on the face of the earth. . . . Buy a reservation by all means, and not try to dispossess honest white men of their property for the purpose of presenting it to the carrion eaters belonging to the Pima tribe."

Poston saw the full impact of the enlarged reservation and could see that Indian-White conflicts would quickly accelerate. As his letter indicated, there were already 78,000 acres in the reservation that had filings pending. The new town of Phoenix was now in the middle of an Indian reservation. Camelback was now Indian land. Poston, who always was a great promoter, put his full energies to the fight.

TERRITORIAL LEGISLATURE WEIGHS IN

Poston's campaign was beginning to pay off by early February 1879. Newspapers in Globe and Tucson weighed in against the enlarged reservation. The 10th Territorial Legislature was in session in Prescott. In just four days a joint resolution was passed and telegraphed to President Hayes in Washington. It must have been some telegram because the legislature appropriated $266 to send the message.

Spring at the Camel's Nose. Photo by J.R. Norton.

FREEMONT TO THE RESCUE

Clearly the telegram had an impact because within one week U.S. Secretary of the Interior Carl Schurz telegraphed Governor Freemont in Prescott saying, "The order will not be construed to interfere with rights acquired by white occupants, and refers only to unoccupied public lands." This did not satisfy Arizona, and the Legislature appropriated $2,000 to send Governor Freemont to Washington to meet with Secretary Schurz and President Hayes to get the order rescinded.

Opposition to the expanded reservation was building at a rapid pace. A mass meeting in Phoenix was reported by the *Salt River Herald* on February 7, 1879, to deal with the matter. The *Miner* fanned the flames with the following headline: "Five Thousand People Homeless! - - One Million Dollars Taken From Settlers - - Agent Stout Triumphant - - Pima Scavengers Rich." According to the *Miner*, it was too much land for "Old Chin-chi-a-cum and his filthy wards numbering about 800 souls."

A DRUMBEAT OF ANTI-INDIAN PRESS

It is hard for us today to realize the depths of anti-Indian feeling among the settlers of the last century. While it is true that some settlers suffered under Indian attacks, more often the case it was the settlers who abused the Indians. The press reports included in this book illustrate the feelings of the day, however inappropriate they may seem to us now.

The drumbeat of opposition continued in the press. On February 15, 1879, the *Salt River Herald* made this statement: "It has been remarked that 'Lo, the poor Indian' is generally opposed to anything like civilization, but a visit to our city would disabuse the mind of any one of the untruth of the assertion, for they can be seen in all their nakedness and laziness hanging around loose in our city at any time. The average civilized Indian has a considerable contempt for manual labor, but he makes a healthy ward for the government, if not employed in 'hair-raising.' "

Confidence in Governor Freemont's influence ran high in Arizona as these comments from the *Salt River Herald* illustrated: "It is. . .but reasonable to suppose that before said order will be executed it will be greatly modified, as we are not prepared to believe that our chief magistrate would willingly inflict injustice upon our early pioneers, or any other class of citizens. . . . Our excellent governor, ripe in experience and thoroughly alive to our best interest, will have an eye single to informing the department and using his executive influence accordingly."

On his way to Washington Governor Freemont stopped for a tour of the Salt River Valley. We know

ABOVE: *Sunset at Bobby's Rock. Photo by J.R. Norton.* INSET: *John C. Freemont. Arizona Historical Foundation, University Libraries, Arizona State University.*

Freemont visited the Scottsdale area, so he passed close to Camelback. On March 1, 1879, Poston resigned his position in the land office in protest to the order expanding the reservation. He said he would have nothing to do with such a large area excluded for settlement.

The Herald (which became the *Phoenix Herald* in 1879) reported on Freemont's progress in Washington, saying that the U.S. President was "quite astonished" at the effect of the order for expanded reservation land and that he and Interior Secretary Shurz were "quite willing" to modify the original order to reduce the reservation.

A TRUE INSIDE TRACK FOR FREEMONT

Letters of protest hit Washington in large volume, not only from Arizonans but from others, as well. Arizonans had confidence in their governor but did not realize the trump card they had in Governor Freemont. Both the President and Secretary Schurz served under Freemont in the Civil War. But even more important, the President's private secretary,

Col. Charles King Rogers, was a secret partner of Freemont's in some Arizona mining ventures.

With this kind of inside influence, Governor Freemont got the job done and on June 14, 1879, President Hayes issued a new order substantially reducing the reservation area. The current reservation reflects that order.

Camelback Mountain and most of the current metropolitan area was removed from the reservation.

Freemont, never one to pass up an opportunity, continued on to New York to raise money for more mining ventures. He did not return to Arizona until August 1879.

Thus, ended one of the most interesting and least told events in Arizona history when the future Phoenix metropolitan area almost became an Indian reservation.

CHOLLA TRAIL

CHAPTER THREE

Phoenix park rangers work on the Cholla Trail. Photo by Bryan Casebolt. OPPOSITE: *Paloverde in bloom. Photo by J.R. Norton.*

The hike to the top of Camelback from the east begins with parking on Invergordon, the major north-south road at the eastern end of Camelback. Parking so far from the trail is the result of a long-fought battle between property owners, who did not want hikers passing close to their homes, a developer who argued that he could not sell home lots near the trail, and the city. So, we spend the first quarter-of-a-mile walk along Invergordon in pleasant neighborhood surroundings. White oleander flowers along the path, although not native to Camelback, provide a vibrant display. On the left is the Phoenician Resort's golf course and beautiful desert plantings. We turn to the west on Cholla Lane, where another quarter-mile walk brings us to the trailhead.

ON REMNANTS OF THE INGLESIDE TRAIL

The Cholla Trail follows the remnants of the first developed trail up Camelback, which was built by the The Ingleside Club (the Valley's first important resort). The club worked hard to popularize the mountain. By 1912 Ingleside had developed a scenic trail up the northeastern side of Camelback to a sad-

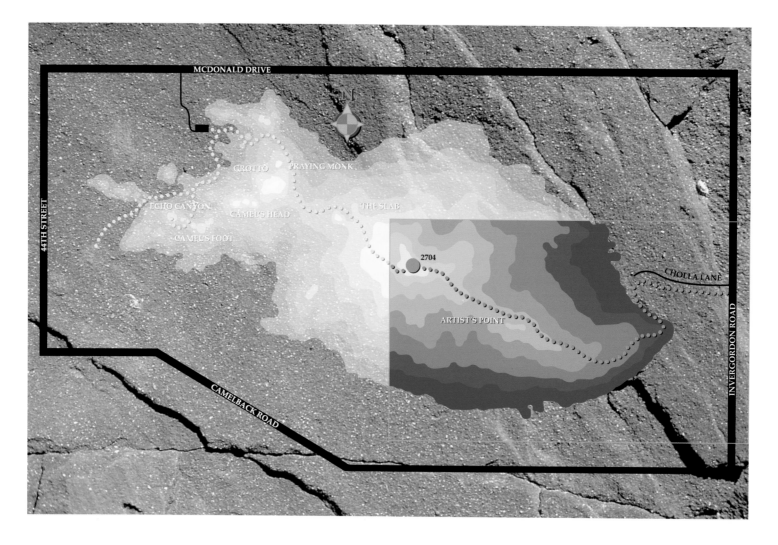

dle between the main hump of the Camel and a smaller hump on the eastern end of the mountain. The Ingleside scenic trail and Camelback were described in glowing terms in *Arizona* magazine: "Phoenix, the queen city of the Great Southwest has, just near enough to have the right effect, a mountain so picturesque and impressive as to be already famous.

"The striking resemblance to a sleeping camel, of this grim and grand old granite mountain, is the first thing that greets the eye of the traveler. . .

"This new Ingleside Trail, midway between Apache Trail, and the trails of the Grand Canyon is the one trail that shows in startling and vivid contrast the old and the new West. . . . By easy stages Artist Point is reached—the most wonderful viewpoint on the mountain. . . . Nowhere are the conditions more perfect to produce these marvelous combinations of color than in Arizona where we find the most striking example in the coloring of the Grand Canyon, the Painted Desert and the view from the Artist's Point."

While today most observers don't put Camelback in the Grand Canyon category for scenery, it's clear that turn-of-the-century Phoenix boosters didn't shy from the comparison. On the other hand, modern

media with all of its artificial and impressive special effects has probably numbed us from seeing the beauty in our own back yard.

GAINS AND LOSSES ON THE CHOLLA TRAIL

As we hike this traditional way to the summit of Camelback, we will follow roughly along the ridge of the mountain from the Camel's tail to the summit. This path has been used for decades. At some undetermined time, probably decades ago, the trail was marked with a series of blue dots spray-painted intermittently onto the rocks leading to the summit, showing the hiker the rough trail that should be followed along the upper rocky slopes of the mountain.

During the original "Save Camelback" campaign, no effort was made to secure trail access from either end of the mountain. In the words of Mrs. Kober in her letter to the original Camelback Mountain foundation members, she said, "After all, our main purpose was to preserve our famous Camel silhouette." In 1971, Charles Christensen wrote to Mr. C.H. Alberding, President of Alsonett Hotel, owner of Jokake Inn, asking that he contribute the land held by Jokake above the 1,800 foot level. Alberding

Spring on the Cholla Trail. Photo by J.R. Norton.

responded that he did not wish to contribute the land but would consider an exchange if the city provided a bridle path that circled the entire mountain. This, of course, was impossible for the city to accomplish because homes already blocked much of the land which would have been required to put a bridle path trail around the mountain. The upper slopes were too steep for a trail around the mountain, particularly the head of the mountain, which would have been impossible for any trail.

By 1975, Alberding was looking for additional zoning to expand the resort or to make his property more saleable. City officials requested Alberding consider providing some type of easement for a trail to the summit from the east end of the mountain. In an April 2, 1975, letter to Alberding, Charles Christensen, director of Parks & Recreation, suggested that Alberding dedicate the land above 1,800 feet as a permanent open space. The city in turn would give him credit on zoning for the number of units that could have been built on that land and that he further provide an easement for a trail that would connect with the trail that had developed over the years by hikers going to the top of Camelback from the east.

By 1985, Alberding had sold the properties to the First Phoenician group which sought additional zoning rights for the property. As a condition of that agreement, the city stated that it would require an easement for a trail to the top, and in fact an agreement was finally reached on January 30, 1985. The agreement provided, among other things, that a trail easement to the top would be given to the City of Phoenix.

Finally, on October 28, 1987, the City of Phoenix authorized an agreement for public access for a hiking trail and a parking lot off Cholla Lane, which would give the city permanent access from the east for hikers to use. In the early years it did not receive great usage, but in time the usage accelerated. The city made no effort to police the area as it did in the Echo Canyon area with the gates being closed at night. So, the parking lot area and the trail head became a popular gathering place at night for young people to drink beer, neck, and watch the city lights. The residential lots near the parking lot for the Cholla Trail did not sell well. This was due in part, no doubt, to the activities of evening parties at the trail head rather than hikers.

By 1995, the Cholla Trail had become very popular and large numbers of cars were parking in the neighborhood. The original parking easement only provided about 10 parking spaces for hikers. On weekends as many as 50 to 100 cars would be parked in the neighborhood and evening revelers left their trash and even graffiti in the neighborhood. The owner of the lots around the trail head in an effort to improve the salability of the lots, hired an attorney and filed documents with the city claiming that the city's failure to properly supervise the activity around the trail head was a breach of the original agreement and therefore as far as the landowner was concerned the easement for the trail was terminated.

There is no question that the city had taken a casual approach and did not even apply the evening closure steps implemented at the Echo Canyon Park. In addition, the usage of the trail had grown to the point where there was clearly a conflict between the neighbors and hikers. The conflict was compounded by the evening parties of the teenagers enjoying the city lights.

THE CHOLLA TRAIL CLOSES

There ensued a number of acrimonious hearings before the City of Phoenix Parks Department. Dozens of hiking enthusiasts appeared and pled for the cause of public access for a trail to the top of Camelback from the east end of the mountain. Irate homeowners complained of the evening parties and thoughtless hikers who left trash or otherwise interfered with the quiet of the neighborhood. At times the hearings reached a shrill level with some homeowners claiming fears of life and limb due to the actions of hikers or others using the mountain. In effect, the hikers became scapegoats for the evening teenage drinking parties. Unfortunately, the city had taken no action to curb the evening parties.

A CITIZENS' COMMITTEE JOINS THE FRAY

A citizens' committee was established, including representatives from the neighborhood and from the Phoenician Hotel and other interested public members. I was asked to serve as a member of that committee and we continued on with a number of committee hearings at which the level of rhetoric continued at an emotional pitch with both hikers pleading for access and homeowners begging for protection from neighborhood interference. There seemed little ground for compromise. The staff report on the trail use impact analysis for the Cholla Trail ad hoc committee had on its cover this quote from Aldo Leopold in 1948: "Public policies for outdoor recreation are controversial. Equally contentious citizens hold opposite views on what it is and what should be done to conserve its resource base . . . a given policy may be true for one, but false for another." This observation seemed equally applicable in 1995.

The hikers and climbers who begged for continued public access seemed to indicate that the impact of the hikers was relatively minor on the mountain. On the other hand, neighborhood activists claimed that the trail used by hikers was destroying the mountain without considering what impact the construction of their houses on the slopes of the mountain may have been or what continuing impact the continuing urbanization of the mountain might have on the environment. The city staff report concluded that the adverse impact of the hikers on the mountain was negligible but did admit that the city had not spent the money to build the trails to the best

Camelback cholla. Photo by Bryan Casebolt.

standards and that, in fact, the trails had simply more or less developed by hiker use with the exception of the volunteer efforts to improve the Echo Canyon Trail.

Based on a review of aerial photographs of Camelback Mountain from 1971, 1990, 1991 and 1995, the Parks Department concluded that there was no perceptible change in vegetation density outside of the trail corridors. Furthermore, they concluded that the vegetation and "the drainage areas in the mountain continued to have healthy stands of paloverde and mesquite trees. These are the predominant trees of the plant association and provide the primary food and cover for the wildlife."

The other plants on the mountain seem to be sustained in a normal manner and did not seem to have had any adverse impact due to the heavy use of the summit trails by hikers. The most significant environmental damage to the mountain resulted from the increased home construction which reduced the natural plant and animal habitat. Based on this

ABOVE: *Cholla flower. Photo by J.R. Norton.*
LEFT: *Gamble's quail. Photo by Paul Berquist.*

ABOVE: *Camelback lichen. Photo by J.R. Norton.* OPPO-SITE: *Phoenician golf course. Photo by Bryan Casebolt.*

analysis the City of Phoenix Parks Department concluded that with proper trail construction, regular maintenance and proper management control the summit trails could handle the existing traffic and reasonable growth without degradation of the mountains existing plant and animal life.

This conclusion of course did not satisfy the homeowners, whose desire was to reduce, if not eliminate, usage of the mountain by the hikers. In any case, the homeowners on the east end of the mountain hoped that the Cholla Trail would be closed and all of the hikers would be forced to use the Echo Canyon Park access to the summit. Numerous hearings followed in front of both the City of Phoenix Parks board and the ad hoc committee of which I was a member. Representatives of hikers and climbers came to plead for increased access for the public and homeowners spoke emotionally of the adverse impact on their neighborhoods due to hikers.

The final conclusion after several months of effort was for the city to attempt to negotiate a new trail right-of-way from the Phoenician Hotel which would

divert traffic away from the subdivision of undeveloped lots and minimize the impact on the neighborhood. Parking would be moved to Invergordon and a trail on the side of Cholla Lane would provide access for hikers, and minimize the impact on the existing homeowners. The compromise required new trail construction so the Cholla Trail was officially closed. Still, that did not deter the climbers who still everyday made their pilgrimage to the summit of Camelback via the old trail.

AGREEMENT FOR A MODIFIED TRAIL

The agreement between the City of Phoenix and the Phoenician was reached in early 1998, and was celebrated by dignitaries with great fanfare. Construction began in earnest to complete the new trail on the east end of the mountain. The H.I.K.E.R.S. Group, led by Phil Richards, put in a tremendous amount of volunteer effort in helping to keep the trail open and build the new alignment. The pool of volunteers was between 125 and 150 people. With the trail open in 1998, there seems to be a truce between the hikers and the homeowners on the east end of Camelback. As has been the case with the mountain over the past several decades, the resolution of the Cholla Trail dispute ended in a compromise which seemed to work reasonably well. Neither side got all they had hoped for, but access to the summit of Camelback remained open to the general public on the tail of the mountain.

I recently spoke to one of the closest neighbors on Cholla Lane about the new trail arrangement. She said it was working well and that they felt no adverse impact from the new trail arrangement.

A WIN FOR H.I.K.E.R.S AND HOMEOWNERS

The H.I.K.E.R.S Group was particularly pleased with their acronym, which stands for Hikers Interested In Keeping Everyone's Rights Secured. It was the H.I.K.E.R.S. Group that fought to maintain public access, that mobilized public support, that prepared leaflets which were left by the water fountain at the start of the Echo Canyon trail, and that mobilized hundreds of mountain users to appear at public meetings asking for continued public access from the east end of Camelback.

The homeowners were partial winners, as well, as they achieved a change in the route of the trail. In the final sense everyone won, as the new trail is much better channeled and confined. The experience of the

Strawberry hedgehog. Photo by J.R. Norton.

National Park Service often proved a well built and maintained trail tends to minimize impact on any natural environment as the hikers and climbers are channeled in a narrow corridor. When development is left to the random paths developed by different hikers, there tends to be a spider web style of many trails generally going in the same direction.

UP THE CHOLLA TRAIL TO THE TOP

Once past the houses and golf course, the trail starts out slowly, winding shallowly around the golf course and surrounded on both sides with abundant desert growth. Large saguaros greet hikers. A gila woodpecker is building a home in one of the saguaros. It is late spring, and the saguaros are ready to bloom with the beautiful, white official state flower of Arizona. Paloverde trees, brittlebush, creosote and bursage, in full bloom, cover the eastern slopes of Camelback. One-quarter mile into the trail, the trail begins to ascend more steeply. The McDowell Mountains to the northeast provide a spectacular view on the horizon and the green of the golf course and the dense foliage of the urban development below provides a verdant view of Scottsdale. The new trail built by the City of Phoenix Parks, Recreation and Library Department, with volunteer help from the H.I.K.E.R.S. Group, is outstanding.

URBAN DEVELOPMENT MEETS CAMELBACK

As we look out onto the Valley, with a seemingly endless vista of urban development in several directions, it is good to remind ourselves that modern development of Arizona only got its start in the mid-1800s. The driving force for development of the West was the California Gold Rush. With the gold rush in full swing, it's not surprising that Arizona would start to pique the interest of prospectors.

Two of the early prospectors were Charles Poston and Herman Ehrenburg who found rich ore near Tubac in 1854. Poston, called the father of Arizona, was a consummate promoter and had more gall and initiative than the next five most important men in Arizona's history combined. As we will later see perhaps his most important contribution to the development of Arizona is little-known.

After his strike Poston traveled to the Eastern money centers and convinced investors to fund his mining and exploring company.

In Tubac he not only ran the mining company but also appointed himself "alcade," which embodied both civil and religious authority. He meted out civil justice and also married couples and baptized the children. In short, Poston was the benign dictator of Tubac.

The Civil War slowed development in Arizona, but after the war settlement accelerated as did conflicts with the Indians.

While metropolitan Phoenix dominates the state today in post-Civil War times, the mining and ranching towns were where the action was.

JOKAKE INN

Artist Jessie Benton Evans came to Arizona in 1911 and purchased 40 acres on the southern slopes of Camelback for $40 per acre. The property had an existing frame house on it and Mrs. Evans, who had a cosmopolitan flair, planned to convert it to an Italian villa.

The 1919 official state ownership map shows J.B. Evans as owner of 40 acres, but much of the land around Camelback shows no ownership. In terms of development in 1919, there were a few homesteaders' shacks and occasional houses on winding dirt roads. A primitive dirt road circled around

Camelback Mountain.

When Madame Evans moved to Arizona, she was already a well-known and accomplished artist. She spoke five languages fluently and had translated and illustrated "Romeo & Juliet" from Italian to English while in Italy. Evans and her husband, Denver, brought support for and interest in the arts to the Valley. She held weekly gatherings, which she called "salons," at her home, open to anyone interested in the arts. The salons included musical programs, dramatic readings and other artistic activities.

Jessie's son, Robert, an architect, moved his family to Arizona for his health. Robert and his wife, Sylvia, drove to Arizona in a 1922 Hudson with all their luggage and three children. Mrs. Evans gave her son and daughter-in-law 12 of her 40 acres. Robert designed and built a home on his property. Robert Evans was fascinated by Hopi design and building style so he used both Native American materials and craftsmen in the construction. He gained the nickname "Adobe Bob."

ABOVE: *The Royal Palms, circa 1947.* RIGHT: *Jokake Inn, circa 1946. McLaughlin Collection.*

Two views of the Phoenician from the Cholla Trail. ABOVE: *Photo by Bob Rink.* OPPOSITE: *The Phoenician, Jokake Inn and Papago Park. Photo by J.R. Norton.*

THE JOKAKE TEA ROOM

Sylvia Evans, together with her friend, Lucy Cuthbert, decided they wanted to do something interesting with their lives, "something on their own." The "something" they settled on was a tea room at Sylvia's new home near Camelback.

The two young entrepreneurs did their decorating. They got craftspersons from the nearby Salt River and Gila River Indian communities to make their pottery. They incorporated Hopi kachina dolls and cactus into the architecture and landscape. They hung Mexican red peppers on the patio and used Mexican chairs and designs. The decor was "Southwestern." Their first employee, a Mexican boy, was dressed to resemble a well-dressed Native American, with a red velvet jacket, white pants, moccasins, Indian jewelry and a red headband.

JOKAKE—MUD HOUSE

When asked for the name of the new tea house by the society editor of the Phoenix newspaper, Lucy Cuthbert asked a Hopi man working in the yard what he called an adobe house. He answered, "Ah, mud house—Jokake." Sylvia Evans and Lucy Cuthbert opened their tea house in 1927. The tea house was an instant success. Guests came from all over the Valley. Nearby Ingleside was a big source of customers. Soon lunch, dinner and more costumed Mexicans were added.

As more and more guests requested overnight accommodations, the pair decided to convert Jokake to an inn. Bob started Evans Construction Company. With their interest in Mexican adobe growing, they traveled to Mexico to learn more about it. They started adding buildings and by 1929 four "Pima" cottages were finished, bringing the inn's capacity to fifty guests.

Horseback riding was the most popular Jokake activity, with breakfast rides and desert rides to Echo Canyon. The riding became so popular that Evans purchased 160 acres on the slopes of the McDowell Mountains—three hours by horseback to the northeast.

Bob Evans designed and built the "Bunk House" with accommodations for eight on the McDowell property. Guests would ride to the Bunk House for

lunch or an overnight stay.

Jokake had a genuine Western flavor. The Evans let the local Native Americans build a wickiup near the Inn's entrance gate where they sold pottery and baskets. Indians in their traditional garb became a colorful trademark for Jokake.

Jokake catered to many famous guests, including Vincent Astor, opera great John McCormick, architect Frank Lloyd Wright, Ronald Coleman, Joel McCrea, Zza Zza Gabor, Hedy Lamarr, Tallulah Bankhead, Milton Berle, Ginger Rogers and an Arabian prince.

Sylvia Evans Byrnes commented on Wright in her published history of Jokake, entitled *Jokake Inn*: "One day as he sat playing the piano in a deserted lounge area of Jokake Inn, I said, in an effort to be sociable, 'My, I didn't know you played.' " " 'Humph,'" came Wright's abrupt reply, "'I play as well as your mother-in-law paints, certainly.' "

Byrnes did every job, including chamber maid and waitress. She recalls receiving a 50-cent tip from famous Chicago architect Jarvis Hunt.

ABOVE: *Creosote, saguaros and paloverde near the Cholla Trail.* LEFT: *Paloverde flower. Photos by J.R. Norton.*

JOKAKE SCHOOL FOR GIRLS

In 1932, another dimension was added to Jokake Inn with the opening of the Jokake School for Girls. The school was run by Barbara and George Ashforth, daughter and son-in-law of Sylvia and Bob Evans.

The goal was to have a truly exclusive school, so they hired Lilias Sebastián Billas to be Head Mistress. She had previously been the Head Mistress at the Cathedral School in Florida.

In spite of the steep tuition—$3,500 to $4,000 per year—the school grew quickly and became an accredited prep school. The school had one teacher for each four students.

Jokake School for Girls offered grades 5-12 and college prep and was limited to 40 students.

Besides academic work, there were many sports activities including horseback riding, tennis, archery, basketball and badminton.

Some of the girls who attended included the daughters of Frank Lloyd Wright, Frank Brophy, John C. Lincoln and J.C. Penny.

Dorm rooms were elaborate and seemed more like a resort than a school. The faculty included well-known people such as Madame Redeuilh, a fellow at the Sorbonne and Beth Blace, an accomplished artist.

In spite of the Depression, Jokake continued to grow, reaching a capacity of 100 guests by 1943.

That same year, Bob and Sylvia Evans divorced. She retained Jokake and Evans built another resort, Paradise Inn, on his mother's remaining property. New partners joined Sylvia. They were Tom Darlington, Otto Utzinger, George Ferris, Al Moriarity and Ronald Byrnes, who she married.

The girls' school was closed in 1945 as Jokake needed more space for expansion.

PARADISE INN

Paradise Inn opened shortly after World War II by Bob Evans. It opened with only the first floor available for occupancy. Bob Evans designed, built and managed the resort. Its marketing brochure touted the Inn as luxurious and a relaxing place for only the most elite of guests. In fact, only those people deemed socially fit and healthy by management were allowed to "find pleasant association with the other guests." Hotel literature made it clear that evidence of good health might be required before a

ABOVE: *Creosote flowers.* BELOW: *Creosote seeds. Photos by J.R. Norton.*

guest could register at the Paradise Inn.

In 1952, Jokake was sold to Charles Alberding. His firm, Alsonett Hotels, had a strategy of buying aging elegant resorts and milking them while investing little in improvements and renovation. He also acquired all the Evans holdings, including Paradise Inn and Valley Country Club—315 acres total.

NIXON'S MOUNT RUSHMORE

During President Richard Nixon's tenure in the White House, someone noticed that the lower rocks of Camelback, as seen driving west on McDonald Drive, bore a striking resemblance to the profile of

Richard Nixon's facial profile on Camelback, as published in The Arizona Republic *in 1973.*

the President's face. *The Arizona Republic* published a picture of the Nixon profile on Camelback. Camelback will probably have to remain as Nixon's only "Mount Rushmore."

THE PHOENICIAN

The most imposing current development on Camelback is the 640-room Phoenician resort. It covers 250 acres on the southeastern slopes of Camelback. The Phoenician exudes opulence. The grounds are lush with fountains, waterfalls, 27 holes of beautifully manicured golf course, and a cactus garden that rivals leading botanical gardens, complete with cacti flown in from around the world. The awards received by the hotel cover eight pages. It is listed in the top ten resorts of the world, as well as number three of the top U.S. mainland resorts, and in the top 25 of 100 best hotels, and on and on. The Phoenician in 1998 comprises the lands once occupied by Jokake Inn, Paradise Inn, Valley Country

Club and Maine Chance.

Rates during the winter season range from $410 a night for the standard room to $1,225 for a suite to about $4,400 for a presidential suite. Even with these rates in 1998, the hotel was running nearly full during most of the winter season.

The story of the development of the Phoenician is one of the most unusual and interesting stories in the history of Camelback Mountain. Camelback has seen many series of ups and downs in the real estate market. Often, those who set out to develop on Camelback saw their dreams dashed by the cycles of the real estate market only to have subsequent owners harvest the full benefits of their earlier dreams. The Phoenician is perhaps the most vivid example of how the real estate cycle ups-and-downs can yield harsh results for some and bonanzas for others.

The Phoenician was the brainchild of Charles Keating. The colorful chairman of American Continental, a savings-and-loan holding company, Keating was the most controversial individual in the savings-and-loan crisis of the late '80s and early '90s. His California and federal criminal trials were among the most well-publicized in U.S. legal history and the subsequent reversal of those convictions one of the more ironic twists in this debatable chapter of U.S. financial history. Even though the Phoenician represents the concept and execution in detail of Charles Keating's vision, the press kit and materials provided by the hotel's new owner, Sheraton Resorts, has no mention of Keating or his role in developing the resort.

THE PHOENICIAN, ACCORDING TO CHARLIE

As the Phoenician's press kit failed to even mention Charles Keating, I wanted to hear his side of the story.

In 1998, he had been released from federal prison after serving four and one-half years on federal charges arising out of the failure of Lincoln Savings. With both his California state and federal convictions reversed, he was facing at the age of 72 either new trials or a chance to get on with his life. He suggested we meet at the Phoenician. He walked in the main entrance dressed in casual but stylish clothes. He looked the part of a successful developer who was just as much at home, as if he still owned the Phoenician.

We sat down in the lobby and for a couple of hours recalled the development of the Phoenician. He had built the Crescent Hotel on Northern Avenue near the Black Canyon Freeway and he learned that Charlie Alberding, who owned Jokake Inn and

The Phoenician Hotel with Allan Houser sculpture in the left foreground.

Paradise Inn, wanted to lease his property on the eastern end of Camelback Mountain. Eventually he had to meet with Alberding himself to close the deal. They met at the Royal Palms for dinner in 1985. Alberding talked tough but clearly wanted to do a deal and Keating said he agreed, more or less, to Alberding's price.

WHY CAMELBACK MOUNTAIN?

I asked Keating why he chose Camelback Mountain as a site for such a grand resort.

"It's the best location in the United States for a hotel," Keating told me. "The land was in the shadow of Camelback Mountain. It was a one-of-a-kind site, and I could not find any other piece of land that good in the entire United States."

His original idea was not to build the finest resort in the world but rather an upper-end resort along the lines of The Arizona Biltmore in Phoenix.

TAX REFORM CHANGES THE GAME

About a year into the project, the Tax Reform Act of 1986 changed everything for the developers of commercial property. Keating had not planned to own the hotel.

Keating remembers the moment: "I said to myself, 'What do I do with a half-built hotel?' The odds are it will be a failure if it is just another ordinary hotel."

The project seemed to make sense before the tax law changes occurred in 1986, and others had been successful with developments of the type Keating envisioned. He said he was convinced that the growth of Phoenix would never quit and that there was no real top-notch hotel that would appeal to the

top one-quarter percent of the population. So, Keating changed strategies. His new goal, he said, was to build the "best hotel in the world."

ON-SITE MANAGER

"We needed major changes. If I did not get results, I knew I would fail," Keating said. "I terminated the architects and I hired Elliott Rumble, who became the architect on site with three assistants. I knew I had to virtually change the entire project midway in the construction if I was to shift from an upper-end nice hotel to the top hotel in Phoenix and one of the top hotels in the entire world." We hired Anukanuhi Anau, who had been trained at the University of New Zealand in horticulture. He had a good eye and brought 115 Tongan workers who even slept on the job site."

In 1988, they worked around the clock. "We brought in a 'SWAT' team who reported to me. We had walkie talkies. I could be on any part of the job within five minutes. I had to make all sorts of changes. I decided on the room sizes. I changed the bathrooms. I tore off facades. I simplified the design. I increased the number of swimming pools from four to seven. I put in the Mother-of-Pearl pool, which turned out to be one of the main attractions of the hotel. I did not take any guff from anyone. They had to do it our way. There were all sorts of problems on the site. People were fighting. At one time there were 1,200 people on the job, then 800, then 600, then 400."

Also scattered throughout the resort are the world-famous sculptures of the late Chiricahua Apache artist Allan Houser.

The RTC took over the hotel in November of 1989 and it became known as "Club Fed." The RTC later

sold its 55 percent interest in the Phoenician to the Kuwait Investment Organization (Keating's minority partner in the project) for $115 million.

At $270 million, the Phoenician was the most expensive development ever built on Camelback. Charles Keating had a vision of creating one of the best resorts in the world. By any objective measure, he succeeded in his goal. But his financial results were not so favorable. Like so many Camelback developers before him—Russ Tatum, Duncan MacDonald and others, the forces of the real estate cycle overwhelmed the Phoenician. Keating feared when building the Phoenician that it would be a subsequent owner that would reap the harvest from the seed he planted.

A NEW OWNER AND PLANS FOR EXPANSION

The ITT Sheraton Hotel chain purchased the Phoenician from the Kuwaitis in April 1994. The new owners quickly developed plans to expand the hotel.

ABOVE: *Dormant Resurrection plant on Camelback Mountain. Photo by J.R. Norton.* RIGHT: *Barrel cactus. Photo by Bryan Casebolt.*

Resurrection plant after a rain. Photo by J.R. Norton.

In August 1994 the Phoenician purchased the 110-acre Maine Chance Spa for just over $9 million cash.

The Phoenician proposed to build up to 100 additional casitas and seven more holes of golf. The expansion would include a 20,000 square foot outdoor pavilion, more parking and spa facilities, along with 78 more casitas.

Nearby homeowners fought the golf course, as it would exceed the height limit for development on the mountain. One of my close friends, Dennis Hopper, has resided more than twenty years across from the site of Maine Chance. He welcomed the golf course as a neighborhood improvement but Dennis Hopper has a discerning eye and was responsible for major improvements in the original zoning for the Phoenician. He had organized neighborhood opposition and printed signs for the neighborhood, which read, "Save the rabbit, save the quail, and don't forget the camel's tail."

The city zoning hearing officer ruled that golf courses did not constitute a structure. As part of a compromise, the Phoenician agreed to cut back on some casitas development. The expansion was com-

pleted in 1996 with 40 additional suites and 20 more guest rooms. As in the past, a controversial new development for Camelback ended in a compromise.

THE ARMY COMES TO ARIZONA

As we look at the development around Camelback, it's hard to realize how recently all this has occurred. After the Civil War a significant part of the U.S. Army was moved to Arizona to fight Indians and protect the white settlers. In September 1865 Fort McDowell was established on the Verde River just north of its confluence with the Salt River.

Fort McDowell was really the beginning of modern development in the Salt River Valley that had remained largely unoccupied since the Hohokam had left some 500 years earlier.

The soldiers and horses of Fort McDowell generated a demand for grain. It was Jack Swilling who reorganized the agricultural potential in 1867 when he noticed the ruins of the ancient Hohokam irrigation system. He soon raised $400 in Wickenburg and was at work by the end of 1867 cleaning out the ancient canals and planting wheat and barley. Swilling's ditch ran from about 40th street in Phoenix to 27th Avenue along the northern side of Van Buren Street. Swilling was a former confederate officer, ex-Indian fighter,

prospector, drunk and—by some accounts—a delightful conversationalist. Most accounts give him credit for naming the new settlement "Phoenix."

The 1868 survey only identifies Camelback and the Phoenix Mountains to the north as "high and precipitous mountains"— "unfit for cultivation." The Papago Park area is only described as "Rocky Buttes." The road from Wickenburg to Fort McDowell is shown near the Papago Buttes but no other trails or roads are shown. There is no specific mention of Camelback Mountain.

By 1870, the population was six women and 164 men. The national depression of 1873 caused cutbacks in mining operations, military contracts and temporarily brought development to a halt.

The first newspaper was the *Salt River Herald,* founded in 1878. An early issue stated "the growth of the town has not been feverish nor of mushroom order, but it has steadily and heartily improved."

It is hard for us to realize today how insignificant a place Phoenix was in the 1870s and how modest its prospects seemed to those first residents. Its economic viability was dependent on providing food and other supplies to the men and animals of the U.S. Army.

AN UNUSUAL VIEW TO THE EAST

As we walk up the trail, we're in the midst of a huge field of desert flowers. At about three-eighths of a mile, we reach the ridge of the Camel's tail. The view below is of downtown Scottsdale to the east. What makes the view of Scottsdale startling is that the city ends abruptly on its eastern boundary with a clear line dividing houses and open green fields for miles beyond.

Pima Road is an appropriate name because it is the border of the Salt River Pima-Maricopa Indian Community. Most people don't know and most histories of Arizona take little note of the fact that the Pima-Maricopa Indian Community at one time encompassed about one million more acres, engulfing almost the entire Phoenix urbanized area.

BOULDERS GALORE

Granite boulders cover the Camel's tail. A thicket of bursage, brittlebush and creosote blankets the sandy, red ground. Cacti are diverse, ranging from an occasional barrel cacti, to giant saguaros to buckhorn cholla to pincushion cacti.

At the half-mile mark the trail continues up a broad boulder field along the rounded lower slopes of the hump. The black patina on the granite boulders creates a wonderful contrast to the green of the desert plants. The air is full of calls from the desert birds. At the three-quarter-mile mark, we're looking directly over the remnants of the old Jokake Inn and the Phoenician Resort, with its golf courses, massive swimming pools and elaborate plantings.

EL ESTRIBO—HIDEAWAY PAR EXCELLENCE

In 1930, the Evans family built a home designed by architect Neil Gates. They called it "Casa de la Montaña," or House of the Mountain. The adobe home was a combination of pueblo and Monterey design.

The name was later changed to El Estribo (The Stirrup) when it was used for guest rooms.

Originally part of Jokake Inn, El Estribo, adjacent to the Phoenician, operated as a small lodge during the 1950s and '60s. An advertisement in the 1950s described El Estribo as, "Off the beaten path away from the traffic noise. A beautiful resort on the south slope of Camelback Mt. surrounded by green lawns

ABOVE LEFT: *Jack Swilling, circa 1880. Arizona Historical Foundation.* LEFT: *Couch's spadefoot toad. Photo by Paul Berquist.* OPPOSITE: *Artist's Point. Photo by Bob Rink.*

LEFT: *Mamie Eisenhower's pink bedroom at Maine Chance.* RIGHT: *Mamie Eisenhower's sitting room at Maine Chance. Arizona Republic, February, 16, 1959.*

and riotous flowers. Of Spanish Colonial design it features spacious well-appointed rooms, luscious food, heated pool and all desert activities. Limited to congenial guests who desire rest and relaxation." Perhaps El Estribo's most famous guest was Massachusett's U.S. Senator Ted Kennedy, who reportedly spent a month in seclusion there after the events at Chappaquiddick. Almost bulldozed in 1984 El Estribo has now been restored and is a private residence.

MAINE CHANCE

In the early '50s, Elizabeth Arden acquired about 110 acres on the southeastern slopes of Camelback for her beauty resort, Maine Chance. For the next three decades the Maine Chance was probably the most famous beauty resort in the world, hosting the rich and famous women from around the world for rest and rejuvenation.

Elizabeth Arden was born Florence Nightingale Graham in 1891 in Woodbridge, Canada. She briefly followed her namesake in nursing but soon found she preferred health maintenance over treating ill-

ness. Her various jobs included a stint in a dentist's office, which taught her about bone structure and their muscles. Later, she worked with her brother at a British cosmetics firm in New York where she learned facial massage.

After a few years, Elizabeth started her own beauty treatment business with $6,000 borrowed from her brother. She opened in a two-room suite on Fifth Avenue in New York offering beauty treatments. About this time she became "Elizabeth Arden." She never legally changed her name but the business name stuck. Her facial massage business was booming and soon expanded to Europe and other foreign markets. Her original cleansing cream and skin lotion was a big success. In 1916 she came out with an improved cleansing cream, "Amoretta." The new cream was a big hit and was soon followed by other cosmetics.

Additional salons were opened and she started selling through department stores. Her beauty salons were dubbed "Arden Repair Shops."

In the early 1930s she bought a farm in Maine and started raising horses. She called it Maine Chance because she took a chance on horses in Maine. She later moved her horse operation to Kentucky. In 1947 her horse, Jet Pilot, won the Kentucky Derby. In Kentucky she turned the horse farm into a health and beauty resort. Maine Chance in Kentucky was so successful she decided to expand to Phoenix. The Phoenix property was the estate of William C. Grunow, which included an elaborate mansion with two swimming pools.

Elizabeth Arden hired Frank Lloyd Wright to remodel and develop the property, but she and Wright clashed. Arden fired Wright.

The Phoenix Maine Chance was an instant success. The wealthy women at Maine Chance were pampered with Elizabeth Arden beauty treatments, massages and moderate exercise. The fare was elegant, including such items as Maine Chance souffle and "cactus pear ice milk."

The resort was lavishly furnished with antiques and original art. The grounds were elaborate with cactus and flower gardens, citrus groves, lush lawns and paths to walk around the 110-acre oasis in the desert.

Guests included Mamie Eisenhower, many senators and congressmen's wives and large numbers of Hollywood leading ladies, including Marilyn Monroe. In addition to pampering and weight loss, many Maine Chance visitors came to be "dried out" and "reconstructed."

The maximum number of guests was 70. For many guests a visit to Maine Chance became a yearly ritual. There was a staff of 65 to serve the 70 guests, not including gardeners. Guests were expected to stay on the property except for occasional shopping in Scottsdale.

However, guests were known on occasion to sneak out for a cocktail or some extra calories. In the 1990s Maine Chance was sold to the Phoenician Resort, torn down and converted into a golf course.

The Phoenician now includes most of the southeastern slopes of Camelback.

ON TO ARTIST'S POINT

We continue working our way up the trail, which meanders through lush foliage up the Camel's tail. At the one-mile mark we are well above the houses at the end of Cholla Lane. Houses, by city ordinance, are limited to 1,800 feet above sea level on Camelback Mountain. The McDowell Mountains, Pinnacle Peak, Black Mountains and the Tonto National Forest all lie on a northeastern horizon. Mature little leaf paloverde trees are in full bloom at this elevation.

About one and one-quarter miles up the trail, we cross from the northern side of the Camel's Tail to a low, flat spot where I can see the entire Valley, from north to south.

Near the turn of the century, early hikers called this Artist's Point. Artists, professional and amateur, would ride horses up the trail to this spot. This viewpoint affords a tremendous view of downtown Phoenix, South Mountain and the Estrella Mountains to the southwest. The remnants of the citrus groves on the southern slopes of Camelback in the Arcadia district still remain, as well as a few of the old date palm groves. The name Artist's Point is not known to modern-day hikers.

A MAGNET FOR DEVELOPMENT

Even before the turn of the century, developers and land speculators were attracted to the area around Camelback.

In 1889 the two sections (1,280 acres) just south of

MERRILL MAHAFFEY

Merrill Mahaffey was born in Albuquerque, New Mexico, in 1937, and received his master of fine arts from Arizona State University. He is known for his interpretation of the mountains and canyons of the Four Corners region. In his early work, Mahaffey created abstract paintings. He began to leave abstract art in 1973 and in 1974 received an epiphany. He saw abstract patterns in snow and natural rock surfaces. He decided Nature was, in itself, abstract. He became a contemporary realist. His paintings are in numerous museums and private collections. He says, "Rock, like organic matter, has its own slow-paced life."

—Southwest Art, September 1992.

Looking east to Camelback from near the Arizona Canal, circa 1912. McLaughlin Collection.

Camelback were subdivided by Andrew Barry. Another section just east of Camelback and south of what is now Camelback Road was subdivided by O.P. Ingalls in 1868. By 1908 J. Elliot Coit described the area South of Camelback as ideal for citrus: "The large bare rocks on the hillside heated by the sun during the days, warmed the air as it is drawn down through the groves at night."

But the real growth began to occur after development of the Arizona Canal. The October 1909 issue of *The Border* magazine published in Phoenix had on its cover a picture of a canal with Camelback in the background with this caption: "Scenes in beautiful Salt River Valley where water from the Roosevelt Reservoir is turning the country into a fairyland of greenery."

After World War I, hundreds of acres of citrus were planted in the Arcadia District south of Camelback Road. The southern slopes of Camelback and the Arcadia area attracted many of the leading citizens of Phoenix. In the March of 1919 issue of *Arizona the State Magazine* an article entitled "Arcadia—a Dream" touting the area as a haven for "enterprise and wealth."

One example of that "enterprise and wealth" sprang up with The Ingleside Club, later called the Ingleside Inn.

SHARING HOSPITALITY AT INGLESIDE

The Ingleside Club was built by W.J. Murphy on 800 acres between Thomas Road and Indian School Road, east of 56th Street. Ingleside (taken from the Gaelic meaning fireside) opened in 1908 and was the first major resort connected to the mountain. Ever a promoter, Murphy developed Ingleside Club to help sell property and solicit investors in his ventures. A 1910 issue of *Arizona the State Magazine* shows a picture of Ingleside with the caption "Ingleside Club House, Salt River Valley, Where Many Wealthy Tourists Spend Their Winters." Murphy planted citrus, olives and dates at Ingleside and started an exclusive subdivision. Ingleside was advertised as "a suburban town of rare attractions, fine water, shaded streets, picturesque surroundings."

Murphy's son, Ralph, converted the Ingleside Club to Ingleside Inn in the '20s. Ralph Murphy was the manager of Ingleside and became one of the great promoters of tourism in the Valley of the Sun. The 1921 telephone directory for the southern district of Arizona lists the "Ingleside Club—Scottsdale."

Ralph Murphy promoted the climate and its proximity to Camelback as major selling features. A promotional brochure in the '20s used the caption "Where Summer loves to linger and Winter never comes."

The Ingleside Club worked hard to popularize Camelback Mountain. By 1912 Ingleside had developed a scenic trail up the northeastern side of Camelback to a saddle between the main hump of the Camel and a smaller hump on the eastern end of the mountain.

Along with the Ingleside Club came residential development. The Arcadia District continues to this day.

ARCADIA—A DREAM

The first residential subdivision north of the Arizona Canal near Camelback was Citrus Homes in 1915. This 25-lot development was at the southwestern corner of 56th Street and Camelback Road.

The Arcadia residential district in 1919 marked the beginning of major development efforts near Camelback. Arcadia indeed was a development on a grand scale. The section of Arcadia east of 56th Street and Camelback Road was 23 blocks of four 10-acre lots. The section west consisted of 18 blocks most of which had eight 5 acre lots. The Arcadia town site was north of Camelback Road and west of 56th Street.

The developers also formed the Arcadia Water Company in 1919 and developed pumping plants capable of supplying 2,100 acres with water through a planned underground water system.

By the mid-1920s, the original developers were out of the project. A variety of new owners refinanced and replatted the development between 1926 and 1930. Some of the new subdivisions were Arcadia Estates (1920), Arcadia Replatted (1926), Glencoe Highlands (1928), Alta Hacienda (1929) and Hacienda Allenada (1930). Even though Arcadia was no longer under one developer's control, the name stuck.

An ad in the same magazine proclaimed ARCADIA as "a subdivision which in years to come will be known as far as Arizona is known." The ad promised "40 acres adjoining the mountain will be dedicated as a Park and winding concrete stairway will be built to the top of Camelback and a rock garden built on top." The ad bragged that "every visitor of any consequence who comes to Phoenix for the next 100 years will visit this point—GRAND CANYON and CAMELBACK will be two points of interest."

The name Arcadia came right out of a Webster's dictionary. It meant a region of simple quiet. The developers were making quite a noise about their plans, however. They included Seymour Jordan, M. Krieg and Charles Kaeter, who wanted to built a concrete stairway to the Camelback summit and a rock garden on top. But the Arizona depression of the early 1920s left them with overdue mortgage payments, and they lost the property.

The next owner was Henry Coerver, a Kansas banker. Coerver continued to sell lots in Arcadia. He installed lights on the southern slope of Camelback as a giant billboard to attract customers. It worked.

Coerver built a home at 5005 East Camelback Road in 1925. It was the first major house on the south side of the mountain's slopes. The home is now the Shemer Arts Center and is owned by the city of Phoenix.

Coerver was doing well in the sale of lots in Arcadia, but in 1928 he hit the jackpot. Just two years after completing his new home on Camelback Road, he sold it for a reported price of $50,000 to Charles L. Shur, President of Pennzoil. He also sold home sites to William Blair Buggaley, a prominent official of Cutterick Publishing Company, and Donald B. Douglas, an official of Quaker Oats.

Other wealthy estates also were beginning to spring up. Among them was that of William C. Grunow, in the same area as Coerver's home.

Grunow, a wealthy eastern manufacturer, moved into his new estate on Camelback in 1931. The Wrigley Mansion also sprang up about the same time a few miles west of the Grunow estate. Both are visible from Artist's Point.

Ed Newhall, whose parents' home was south of the Grunow estate, recalls elaborate parties with orchestras being staged at the estate. Grunow's company would go broke during the 1930s, however, and the home became part of the Maine Chance health and beauty resort.

UP THE RIDGE TO THE SUMMIT

The route continues up the rocky ridge of the hump, which now becomes narrower with beautiful views both to the north and the south. Occasionally, both hands and feet are needed to scramble up the rocky ridge. The granite rocks that comprise the hump of the mountain are quite varied with occasional seams of green rock in various textures. The last of the ocotillo flowers provide an occasional

ABOVE: *Camelback's buckhorn cholla bloom in April and May. Native Americans eat the flower buds after steaming them. Photos by J.R. Norton.* OPPOSITE: *On the ridge of the Cholla Trail. Photo by Bryan Casebolt.*

splash of bright red . The trail becomes faint.

The last one-quarter mile along the Cholla Trail to the summit becomes more of a knife-like ridge, with the trail winding back and forth along the rocks at the top of the ridge. A great sheer wall of more than two hundred feet looms—the final challenge before reaching the summit. This wall is home to dozens of cliff swallows, which can be seen darting in front of the wall. Occasionally, their numbers are so large that they create an "avian sonic boom" as they whiz past us.

As always, there is a sense of accomplishment on reaching the summit. The view is well worth the effort. The area on top is large and relatively flat. This makes for lots of conversation. The usual social barriers seem to melt for those on the top of Camelback.

As we are on the highest point in Phoenix, it's a good time to remind ourselves that we are on a sacred mountain. An abundance of worship centers are in clear view around the mountain. To the north, the Franciscan Renewal Center is prominent and to the south the Mount Claret Center, just north of Camelback Road and west of 56th Street, appears as a kind of religious hideaway, which it is.

GERTRUDE DIVINE WEBSTER

As appropriate to her name, Gertrude Divine Webster's home on Camelback eventually became the Mount Claret Center, serving as a Roman Catholic retreat for both the priesthood and lay members.

In the early 1930s, Gertrude Divine Webster, heir to a large Vermont lumber fortune, moved to Phoenix and built a country estate on the southern slope of Camelback. She loved the native plants of Arizona and soon became the president of the Arizona Cactus and Native Flora Society. She planted an elaborate cactus garden on her estate and entertained luncheon and dinner guests at her home with speeches from well-known botanists.

She played a key role in the establishment of the Desert Botanical Garden at Papago Park. While she hobnobbed with the rich and powerful and provided substantial funds for the development of the botanical gardens, Webster had little patience for the local teenagers who enjoyed playing in her cactus garden.

ABOVE: *South Mountain, the Estrella Mountains and downtown Phoenix from Cholla Trail.* OPPOSITE: *Nearing the summit on the Cholla Trail. Photos by Bryan Casebolt.*

Webster had a number of Oriental sculptures in her garden, which prompted the local teenagers to refer to her as "Dragon Lady." The Webster Auditorium at the botanical garden stands as a monument to her civic generosity.

THE SHADY SIDE OF THE MOUNTAIN

As we look down on the houses that surround Camelback Mountain, we are impressed with the sheer size of the structures, particularly those on the northeast slopes in subdivisions restricted to five-acre lots. A new home is being built by professional golfer Hale Irwin, with more than 22,000 square feet. Some nearby houses look and feel more like small resorts than individual homes.

These are modern castles. They are, however, on the shady side of the mountain, and many developers in the 1940s and 1950s considered that land to be undesirable because the mountain shaded the lots from the winter sun, leaving them rather chilly. It's just a little amusing that several of Arizona's richest of the rich are either building or remodeling homes on the shady side of the mountain—land that people a few decades ago considered undesirable. These five-acre lots sell in the range of $2 million to $3 million. Often, the lot includes a reasonably impressive home. These homes are "tear-downs" to make way for the modern castles.

THE SPIRITUAL SIDE OF THE MOUNTAIN

As impressive as some of man's constructions on the mountain are, they all pale into insignificance when compared either in size or beauty to the mountain. Camelback's time is measured in millions or even billions of years. Man's constructs have come and gone. Man's dreams will rise and fall in the mountain's shadow, but the mountain continues.

Some of the saguaros we look at may be approaching 200 years of age. The mountain has been a spot for religious ceremonies that we know of dating back nearly a thousand years. Today, modern pilgrims climb Camelback each day seeking physical and spiritual renewal. Camelback provides the environment; the answers come from within.

Nearing the summit on the Cholla Trail. Photo by Bryan Casebolt.

ROBERT McCALL *"Within Our Reach," commissioned by Honeywell, captures the possibilities of the future as we move beyond today's space frontier. McCall views Camelback every day from his Paradise Valley home. He is America's best-known space artist. The painting asks, "How did the moon get so close?" The answer: Through the ingenuity of man.* OPPOSITE: *View from summit. Photo by Bryan Casebolt.*

EPILOGUE

All the land around Camelback has been subdivided. Only a few vacant lots remain undeveloped and these few lots are being quickly used—usually with homes costing $1 million or more. The parklands have been acquired by Phoenix and good trails are open to the public from both the east and west ends of the mountain. Rock climbers are on the head of the Camel every day enjoying the best-in-town rock climbing in the world.

Camelback is a spiritual and recreational treasure for both residents and visitors to the Valley of the Sun. It would be nice if more of the mountain were included in the park. If the treasures of Camelback had been more widely known, it would have likely been set aside as a national monument. As is so often the case, there has been a compromise between the forces of development and those of preservation. What is left in public ownership is still one of the jewels of Arizona.

Problems remain. Parking lots are often full and neighbors complain that hikers leave trash and are sometimes a disturbance. The Town of Paradise Valley has been relatively hostile to efforts to solve the parking problem. No parking signs have been erected on most streets near the access points to the mountain.

Yet the popularity of Camelback continues to grow. More and more people want to climb Camelback and enjoy the spectacular views of the mountain. It will take cooperation and public money to solve the parking problems.

With usage growing it will take more supervision to avoid adverse impacts on the mountain. Public education about the mountain and its unique resources may help develop more restrained use. Guided tours might also help educate the public about Camelback. As someone who is on Camelback almost every day, I find people very interested in the story of Camelback. Organized tours would probably be well attended. Camelback is a great display of the nature of the Sonoran Desert. We need volunteer nature guides.

The public has a resource of very special value in Camelback. It needs to be used, cared for, explained and preserved for future generations. The public needs to respect the needs of the residents and visitors who also share the mountain. All this takes public money. More rangers should be provided and more funds available for park and trail maintenance and development. In the past, the city of Phoenix has not provided adequate funds to manage a park with such heavy usage. Camelback deserves better.

The full story of Camelback will never be told because it lives on and changes every day. It is my hope this book will help us appreciate Camelback as we continue to shape its history. Camelback is a very special place. It is a sacred place. It deserves to be treated with reverence.

ROCK CLIMBING

CHAPTER FOUR

Technical rock climbing in Arizona got its start on March 19, 1944, when Ray Garner took a group of Senior Scouts to teach them technical climbing on Camelback. Garner, a Grand Teton National Park mountain guide, cinematographer and pilot, soon left for war service as a pilot in the Pacific. After the war, he returned to Phoenix and resumed climbing with the Scouts.

About January 1947, the mountain climbing Kachinas were organized as Senior Scout Outfit No. 1. In addition to the first technical climbing on Camelback, the Kachinas pioneered climbing on other Arizona mountains, such as Saddle Mountain, the Eagletails, the Superstitions, the Kofas and Castle Rock. Garner also had the Kachinas making climbing and other movies. Active early Kachinas included Win Aikin, Robert Brock, Jim Colburn, Ed George, Dick Hart, John Katsenes, Bill McMorris (who would later become editor of *Boys Life*), Bob Owens, Ben and Lee Pedrick. Later Kachinas included John Goodson, Stan Lerch, Gene Lefebvre, Jack Allen and Charlie Scarborough. I joined in 1950 and continued recording Kachina climbs.

The head of Camelback was the primary rock-climbing area for the Kachinas. They completed many first ascents of routes on Camelback. Their names and those that followed in the Kachinas often attached their names to the climbs they pioneered. Thus, we have Pedrick's Chimney and Split, the Hart Route, the George Route and Pateman's Caves.

DEATH ON CAMELBACK

For regular climbers of Camelback, Fire Department rescue squads also are a familiar sight. Groups of a dozen or so rescue workers regularly come to Camelback to hone their skills. The favorite spot for firefighters from all over the Valley is Sugar

Cube Rock or the Rescue Boulder a few hundred feet up the Echo Canyon Trail to the summit. Here, they practice rappelling and using their rescue baskets.

Real rescues are also common on Camelback. One of the first things hikers pass on their way up the Echo Canyon Trail is a helicopter landing pad, and it gets plenty of use. Higher up, reflectors have been embedded in the rocks on the steeper parts of the mountain to help helicopter pilots land for night rescues.

In most years there is more than one death on Camelback. Heart attacks claim more victims than falls from the steep cliffs. Many of the walls of Camelback offer abundant hand and foot holds. Climbing the walls seems like a good idea until you look down and realize a single slip could mean death.

Many accidents occur on a sheer 200-foot cliff called "Suicide." Sometimes inexperienced hikers try to tackle it without proper gear. Climbing down many of these steep slopes is more difficult than getting up, so the most common helicopter rescue is of an inexperienced climber who is stuck on top of some part of Camelback.

During the 1960s the police would call me to do rescues on the mountain. Later, organized rescue teams took over the job.

THE FIRST ASCENT OF THE PRAYING MONK

From the first time that climbers looked at the Monk they had speculated at the prospects of climbing it. A few tried it but after climbing a few feet up they would always turn back. In the 1950s it was thought that the only possible way to scale it was to shoot an arrow over the top with a rope tied to it and prusik (a rope-climbing method) up to the summit.

OPPOSITE: *45th-anniversary climb, celebrating the first ascent in 1951. Photo by Bob Rink.*

UPPER LEFT: *Rescue on Camelback.* LOWER LEFT: *Fire Department trains for rescues.* ABOVE: *Rescue completed.*
Photos by Bryan Casebolt.

I wrote the following account in my climbing journal in 1951: "On December 26, 1951, Guy Mehl and I decided to go out and have a try at climbing the so-called impossible Monk. There is a large detached rock that leans against the Monk on the east side and by going chimney style between this and the Monk we gained access to the face about 30 feet above the base. The first few feet were a little difficult and after climbing about 8 feet above the first piton I thought there was need for more protection and placed another piton in the rock. It was not very good as I could drive it in only a half-inch, but nevertheless it was the best I could do so it would have to do. From this piton I started traversing to the right for about 15 feet. Here I found some small holes in the rock that I could place my feet into while I rested. The climbing above this looked quite difficult for there were no good handholds for about 10 ft. It would have been very dangerous to go on without more protection so I

immediately started looking for a crack to place a piton into. For 20 minutes I looked in vain but finally found a small crack and placed a wedge piton into it.

The next few feet was to be the crucial point of the climb. I climbed 6 feet up and to the left. The rock I was hoping to reach was still about a foot beyond my reach. Below it I could see a small hole where I could place my feet if I could only reach the rock. The only way to reach it was to lunge, and that I did. After pulling myself over the rock the climbing got a little easier, and the last 50 feet was uneventful with the exception of a few crumbling handholds.

At 12:30 I gazed on the summit of the Monk, the prize of Camelback, the impossible Monk. There, I found a belay point on the summit and belayed Guy up. Guy came up the face without any real difficulties.

As soon as Guy reached the top I drove in a long Austrian piton and we belayed each other while on the summit. We built a medium-sized cairn and,

Rock climbing on the head of Camelback. Photo by Bryan Casebolt. OPPOSITE: *45th-anniversary Praying Monk climb, as seen from a helicopter. Photo by J.R. Norton.*

because we had brought no pen no pencil and paper, we each left an identification card in the cairn.

After passing 30 minutes on the summit Guy belayed me down onto the back of the Monk and I drove in two pitons to rappel from, and secured a few strands of nylon sling rope. As soon as this was completed Guy took out the piton on the summit, and we prepared to descend. It was a long rappel and we had to tie two ropes together in order to reach the bottom. The rappel down was very spectacular as part of its overhanging. As we reached the overhang the rope would hurl us into space and we would swing back and forth like a pendulum. When we reached the bottom we were quite relieved, and when we looked back at the imposing Monk, we knew we had really made a climb."

In a recent calendar put out by *Climbing Magazine*, the Praying Monk was listed as one of the classic climbs in America.

Today, better shoes and significantly improved climbing gear and bolts for protection have made the Praying Monk an easier climb than in 1951. The

Monk is now climbed hundreds of times each year and Camelback is probably the best in-town climbing area in the United States.

In the mid-1950s, the Kachinas declined and there was no active organized rock climbing on Camelback until 1961, when the Arizona Mountaineering Club was organized by Bill Forrest, Doug Black, Wally Vegors and Bill Greenwood. The AMC further advanced climbing on Camelback with new and more difficult routes.

the climbing philosophy of the Kachinas was to minimize the use of bolts and artificial climbing aids.

In addition to the 50-odd climbing routes, the rock along the trail to the summit has become a popular bouldering spot. Bouldering is climbing relatively small rocks 10-25 feet—usually without ropes.

The main bouldering area is to the left of the main trail in Echo Canyon Park about one-eighth mile from the parking area. You will often see climbers changing into their rock climbing shoes at the main boulder at the top of the first stairs. Other beginning climbers are learning to rappel on the Search and Rescue (Sugar Cube)

boulder a little further up the trail.

Bouldering enthusiasts have named the principal boulders or routes with names such as No Baloney, Boulder, Rock Pile, Flaming Testicle, and Sugar Loaf. The names change and evolve as new climbers try their stuff.

In the first days of rock climbing in the '40s and '50s we didn't even bother with the boulders. The names of other rocks and walls were different, but that is the beauty of rock climbing and mountaineering—it changes with each generation.

One thing is clear—Camelback Mountain and Echo Canyon Park is probably the finest climbing area inside a major city. I've met climbers from all around the world who have come to enjoy the bouldering or rock climbing on Camelback. I remember meeting a German group who had come to take bouldering pictures for a German magazine.

In December 1996, I organized with members of the Arizona Mountaineering Club a 45th-anniversary climb of The Praying Monk. I was glad to still be able to lead the climb, but that was only possible with the improved climbing shoes and the bolts for protection that have now been installed on the east face of the Monk. I'm sure I could not have repeated the climb with the equipment I first used in 1951.

LEFT: *Climbers celebrate the 45th-anniversary climb of the Praying Monk. Photo by Bob Rink.*
INSET: *Sunset from top of Camel's Head. Photo by Bryan Casebolt.*

ACKNOWLEDGEMENTS

For many years, I have thought about doing a book on Camelback Mountain. Camelback has played an important role in many aspects of my life and continues to inspire me. I climb it almost daily before going to work.

The work to complete the book began in earnest in 1996 with historic research and photography.

THE PHOTOGRAPHERS

In 1996, my longtime friend, photographer John Norton, agreed to help. John and I went on dozens of photographic excursions around and up and down Camelback, taking thousands of pictures of the mountain from almost every conceivable angle. John continued to work with me through the publication of the book. John took more photographs in the book than anyone else. It is particularly appropriate for John to play a key role as his grandfather was part of the party that W.J. Murphy encouraged to locate a dam site on the Salt River around the turn of the century.

Bryan Casebolt moved to Phoenix in 1998 after working several years as a professional photographer in New York. He agreed to help with the photography, particularly with photos on the steeper parts of the mountain. Bryan spent many hours and days with me on Camelback, climbing over nearly every part of the mountain.

Spring 1998 was particularly wet, so the wildflowers on Camelback put on an unprecedented display. This often meant that a particular flower or image was only available for a very brief period. Bob Rink was willing to work during several of those special times, including the photography of the 45th-anniversary climb of the Praying Monk. Photographer Jerry Duchscherer pitched in with some important photos.

Jeff Kida, photojournalist with *The Arizona Republic* and *Arizona Highways,* did excellent work on some of the people shots. Historic photos were largely provided by Dorothy McLaughlin, from the outstanding Herb and Dorothy McLaughlin Collection. Paul Berquist provided superb wildlife photography. John and Gail Driggs photographed waterfalls at their peak.

BOOK DESIGN AND EDITING

After accumulating over 5,000 current and dozens of historic pictures and writing an extensive manuscript of Camelback stories, I went to longtime friend Gary Avey, a former editor of *Arizona Highways* magazine and currently publisher of *Native Peoples* magazine for help in designing and editing this book. Gary agreed to design and edit the book with editorial help from Ben Winton, editor of *Native Peoples,* and Carlos Peinado, *Native Peoples* creative director.

Gary brought a unique background to the task of designing and editing this book. He learned design at the foot of his father George Avey, who was art editor of *Arizona Highways* for more than 30 years. His art legacy also came from his grandmother, Rose Hamilton Avey, who was the first art teacher for the Mesa school district. Gary provided not only artistic talent in book design, but was also a great help in shaping the material into a manageable book.

Gary and I spent many hours in the difficult task of selecting the images for this book, as there are so many beautiful views of Camelback.

Ben and I spent many hours together refining the text to its final form. Carlos added the magic of modern computer technology to format the graphics. Ray Vote Graphics helped design the maps.

RESEARCH

Many people contributed to the research efforts. *The Arizona Republic* gave me access to both their library and their photographic archives. This allowed me to track over many decades almost every *Republic* and *Gazette* article relating to Camelback. This was invaluable.

The staff of the Arizona Historical Foundation provided substantial help. In particular, their collection of the Goldwater papers about the Save Camelback efforts and the historical records relating to the efforts to turn most of Phoenix into an Indian reservation added greatly to the final result.

John Jacquemart did many hours of research on the project, collecting a great deal of information from various sources including official federal and state records and substantial library research. I also

ABOVE: *Ray Garner and the Kachinas filming a movie on Camelback in 1947. Notice the girls carry the packs.*

made important use of the ASU Library, the Phoenix Public Library, the Scottsdale Public Library, the State Capitol Library, the Arizona Collection at ASU and the Arizona Historical Society.

A TEAM EFFORT

The final result was only possible with the combined efforts of the photographers, senior editor Gary Avey, text editor Ben Winton, graphics editor Carlos Peinado and all those who assisted in the research, provided interviews and helped in the research and data collection. I am especially grateful to Evelyn Cooper, director of the Arizona Historical Foundation, the publisher of the book, for her help and encouragement. I will always be indebted to those who provided so much help in bringing this project to completion.

CHAPTER NOTES

The goal of this book is to help those who climb or just look at Camelback appreciate its rich, natural and human history. These are stories, and we jump over a lot of detail. In that spirit, these chapter notes give the basics of the sources.

CHAPTER 1

The descriptions of the sacred history of Camelback are based on discussions with the Phoenix city archaeologist and numerous publications, letters and articles relating either to the Ceremonial Grotto on Camelback or general articles about the religious practices of prehistoric Native Americans.

One of the most important sources was Omar A. Turney's "Prehistoric Irrigation," 1929. This work

CHAPTER NOTES

contains an extensive discussion of the Ceremonial Grotto. This cave has been given several names, such as Camelback Cave and Camelback Salt Cave, but I prefer Turney's "Ceremonial Grotto." Among the many other sources consulted were Frank Mitalsky's article "Ancient Ceremonial Caves of Central Arizona" in the *Arizona Historical Review*, January 1931. *The Arizona Republican*, March 26, 1911 issue, provided helpful early information on the "Ancient Shrine of an Unknown People," and *The Arizona Republic*, June 3, 1959, told the story of a later excavation. I also reviewed ASU's records of their excavation of Camelback Salt Cave.

I have had numerous discussions with Ed Bernbaum about sacred mountains, and he has hiked Camelback with me several times. His book, "Sacred Mountains of the World," Sierra Club Books, San Francisco, 1990, is an outstanding resource for understanding the world's sacred mountains.

The geology of Camelback's creation is based in part on a master's thesis by Gail Cordy, "Environmental Geology of the Paradise Valley Quadrangle," ASU, 1978, and Halka Cronic's "Roadside Geology of Arizona," Mountain Press Publishing Co., Missoula, Montana, 1983, and letters from the Department of Geology at the University of Arizona. The tall tales of the Camel's creation are based on a Bert Fireman column in *The Arizona Republic*, August 5, 1949.

Information on the U.S. Survey of Camelback is based on official records from the Bureau of Land Management in Phoenix. I reviewed copies of the original survey notes. The story of volunteer trail building is based on personal experience and an interview with Paul Diefenderfer.

The Camelback Inn information was taken from various newspaper and magazine articles, personal experiences and recollections and information and literature provided by Camelback Inn. The information relating to the bingo fines came from the Scottsdale Public Library.

Stories of Jack Tatum were based on promotional materials for Tatum's subdivisions, newspaper accounts and Arizona Corporation Commission official records.

The Orme Lewis story was based on my own experience and interviews with Orme Lewis, Jr.

Stories on land sales were based in part on a booklet written for the city of Phoenix Parks, Recreation and Library Department by Martha Shemer.

"Arizona, A State Guide" was compiled by the Writers Program of the Works Projects Administration in the state of Arizona during the Depression of the 1930s. It was sponsored by the Arizona State Teachers College in Flagstaff and published by Hastings House in New York. It provided a wonderful description of Arizona in addition to that of Camelback, which is summarized in this book.

The preservation of Camelback stories are based on my own experiences and contemporary newspaper accounts and a review of the Barry Goldwater papers at the Arizona Historical Foundation and the city of Phoenix Parks Recreation and Library Department records, as well as interviews with many of those involved in the efforts.

The Camelback rattlesnake discussion is based on my own experience. Other references used include Robert L. Smith's "Venomous Animals of Arizona," University of Arizona Press, Tucson, 1982, and Erik D. Stoops and Annette Wright's "Snakes and Other Reptiles of the Southwest," Golden West Publishers, Phoenix, 1993.

Some of the references used for the saguaro discussion include John Alcock's "Sonoran Desert Summer," University of Arizona Press, Tucson, 1990, and "Sonoran Desert Spring," University of Arizona Press, Tucson, 1994.

The tennis ranch stories were based on personal experiences, with additional information provided from *Arizona Republic* articles on Jan. 10, 1990, Jan. 17, 1985, April 12, 1970, and Jan. 25, 1970. Senior Editor Gary Avey worked at the tennis ranch in the 1950s and had useful recollections.

The story of the Royal Palms is based on newspaper articles about Delos Cooke and his original estate and its later conversion to the Royal Palms. I also consulted newspaper articles and biographical information relating to subsequent owners and had discussions with the present owners who converted the Inn to its most recent status.

CHAPTER NOTES

CHAPTER 2

The cane cigarettes pictured on page 76 actually came from the excavation of the Ceremonial Grotto on Camelback. They were photographed by Brenda Shears and Michael Barton of ASU's Anthropology Department. The evidence of the spiritual nature of the Ceremonial Grotto and the sacred cigarettes is well-documented in the chapter, and there are many additional sources which could have been added.

The discussion about the effect of desert rains is based on personal experience. There is a good discussion about desert rains in Joseph Wood Krutch's "The Desert Year," University of Arizona Press, Tucson, 1951.

The many names for the Praying Monk are based on my own readings and conversations with long-time residents who were used to calling it The Old Man of the Mountain and other names. In an article entitled "Monk-e Business," in *Phoenix Magazine*, May 1989, by Edna Evans, also referred to several of these names.

The story of Camelback Castle is based on newspaper accounts and a description in Judy Martin's "Arizona Walls: If Only They Could Speak," published by Judy Martin in Phoenix, 1997.

Information on Cudia City was obtained from the Arizona Historical Society and the Arizona Historical Foundation. Space did not allow for much discussion of Cudia City, but many movies were filmed there using Camelback as a backdrop. Other movies were made north of Camelback during the 1920s, '30s and '40s.

The stories of the animals of Camelback came from personal experience, talks with Camelback residents, the Arizona Game and Fish Department and city of Phoenix Parks personnel. The lists developed by the Arizona Game and Fish Department show many more species than discussed in this book. George Olin's "House in the Sun," Southwest Parks and Monuments Association, Tucson, 1994, was very helpful in the stories about both Camelback's plants and animals.

The stories about wildflowers, mosses, lichens and liverworts are based on my own experiences and also on the following sources: Francis Hamilton's "The Desert Garden: Native Plants of Phoenix and Vicinity," 1933; George Olin's "House in the Sun;" Lyman Benson's "The Cacti of Arizona," University of Arizona Press, Tucson, 1969; Nat Dodge's "Flowers of the Southwest Desert," Southwest Parks and Monuments Association, 1985; Emily Bower's "Shrubs and Trees of the Southwest Deserts," Southwest Parks and Monuments Association, 1993; and Ann North Epple's "A Field Guide to the Plants of Arizona," Falcon Press, Helena, Montana, 1995.

Christmas on Camelback.
Photo by J.R. Norton

The stories about necking on Camelback are based on extensive discussions with mature adults who recall with great delight their teenage romantic experiences on Camelback.

The Duncan MacDonald story is based on interviews with Dennis Hopper, whose father worked for Duncan MacDonald, newspaper accounts and obituaries, and an excellent article in *Scottsdale Scene*, March 1984, by Fran Carlson. In March 1929, the *Arizona Republican* published a story and drawing of his "handsome Spanish-style residence on the side of Camelback."

The story about the Goddard land gift to the city of Phoenix was based on city of Phoenix records and discussions with Terry Goddard, former Phoenix mayor and son of Sam Goddard.

The discussion on plant classifications and plant characteristics are based on my own experiences and a review of numerous nature books, including those already mentioned.

The section on the Arizona Canal was based to a significant degree on Merwin L. Murphy's "W.J. and the Valley," Alhambra, California, 1975.

The Echo Canyon Bowl Association story is based on several newspaper accounts and the records of the Arizona Corporation Commission, as well as interviews with people who recall participating in cultural activities in Echo Canyon.

Material and permission to use the paintings of Maynard Dixon and Gunnar Widforss were made possible by Abe Hays of the Arizona West Galleries.

CHAPTER NOTES

Information on Charles Poston was obtained from the Arizona Historical Foundation and various articles on Poston's life. The Bert Fireman collection at the Arizona Historical Foundation provided useful insights into the 1879 presidential declaration and rescission.

CHAPTER 3

Information on Ingleside Inn was obtained from the Arizona Collection and the Arizona Historical Foundation at the ASU Library. Several articles were reviewed including *Arizona the State Magazine*, December 1910, and *The Arizona Republic*, October 4, 1961, story of Ralph Murphy's death at age 85. A 1910 issue of *Arizona* magazine also provided useful information.

The Cholla Trail story is based on my own experiences as a participant on the city's ad hoc committee and an extensive review of city of Phoenix Parks, Recreation and Library Department files.

The section entitled "Urban Development Meets Camelback" is based in part on Marshall Trimble's "Roadside History of Arizona," Mountain Press Publishing, 1986, and Bradford Luckingham's "Phoenix the History of a Southwestern Metropolis," University of Arizona Press, 1989.

The story of Jokake Inn is based on Sylvia Byrnes' "Jokake Inn: One of the Earliest Desert Resorts," published by Sylvia Byrnes and obtained from the Scottsdale Public Library. I also referred to a March 3, 1972, *Phoenix Gazette* article, as well as other *Republic* and *Gazette* stories. The Scottsdale Public Library's resort files also were helpful.

The Phoenician story is based on personal experience, a review of numerous articles in *The Arizona Republic* and *Phoenix Gazette* and a lengthy interview in spring 1998 with Charles Keating at The Phoenician. There also is an extensive discussion about The Phoenician in Michael Binstein's and Charles Bowden's book "Trust Me," Random House, New York, 1993.

Stories of El Estribo are based on recollections of neighbors, newspaper articles and advertisements. The Scottsdale Public Library proved a good source for El Estribo.

Stories of Maine Chance are based on recollections of neighbors and newspaper and magazine reports. The Scottsdale Public Library had useful information. Also, a June 1997 article in the *Arcadia News* by Annette Makino and a January 1970 article in *Phoenix Magazine* proved helpful.

Use of the paintings by Ed Mell and Merrill Mahaffey were made possible by the Suzanne Brown Galleries. The story of Arcadia is based on numerous newspaper and magazine articles, including *Arizona the State Magazine*, March 1919, subdivision plats and ownership records and city of Phoenix studies.

The stories of Gertrude Divine Webster are based on the spring 1985 *Agave*, the quarterly magazine of the Desert Botanical Gardens, Phoenix, and the *Sonoran Quarterly*, March to May 1994, the bulletin for members of the Arizona Desert Botanical Gardens, Phoenix, Volume 48, Number 1, and an interview with Ed Newhall, who grew up in the area when Mrs. Webster lived on Camelback Mountain.

"The Shady Side of the Mountain" story is based on interviews with longtime Camelback residents.

EPILOGUE

In numerous discussions with city parks officials, it became clear that there are not adequate funds to maintain the parks the city already has. Natural areas still require substantial supervision and maintenance.

CHAPTER 4

Information on the Kachinas is based on personal experience and interviews with many former Kachinas, Kachina journals and my own climbing journals.

Information on Camelback rescues was based on Phoenix city Fire Department records and discussions with rescue personnel on the mountain.

SUMMARY

This book is a compilation of stories, photographs and paintings that relate to Camelback. It is not an attempt to tell the whole story. The nature sections are, by definition, brief and not comprehensive. Camelback's story is the evolution of the Sonoran Desert and its largest city. This book is just a glimpse of that unfolding story.

OPPOSITE: *Coming down.* FOLLOWING PAGE: *Sunset from Camelback. Photos by Bryan Casebolt.*

Camel Back Mountain, near Phoenix, Ar